FACTS AND FIGURES
Basic Reading Practice

Patricia Ackert
Center for English as a Second Language
University of Arizona

illustrated by
Patricia Phelan Eisenberg

NEWBURY HOUSE PUBLISHERS, Cambridge
A division of Harper & Row, Publishers, Inc.
New York, Philadelphia, San Francisco, Washington
London, Mexico City, São Paulo, Singapore, Sydney

Library of Congress Cataloging-in-Publication Data

Ackert, Patricia.
    Facts and figures.

    1. English language--Text-books for foreign speakers.
I. Title.
PE1128.A2975   1986   428.6'4   85-15427
ISBN 0-88377-312-0

Cover by MGT Designs

Book design by Christy Rosso

NEWBURY HOUSE PUBLISHERS
A division of Harper & Row, Publishers, Inc.

Language Science
Language Teaching
Language Learning

CAMBRIDGE, MASSACHUSETTS

First printing: February 1986
8 10 9 7

Printed in the U.S.A.
63-20022

TO THE STUDENT

I hope you enjoy this reading book.
You will learn a lot of English from it.
You can also learn a lot about the world.
Patricia Ackert

CONTENTS

TO THE INSTRUCTOR

This beginning ESL reader is for students who have studied English for five or six weeks and know about 300 words. It teaches about 500 more words. It also teaches the reading skills of comprehension, finding the main idea, and using the context to understand vocabulary items. It is especially suitable for students who plan to attend a university.

An instructor's manual with answers to all the exercises is available. The manual also includes an exam for each unit.

This text is particularly useful for students coming from another alphabet because the texts are short, most of the sentences are short, and there is constant repetition of vocabulary and structures.

Reading Selections. Each of the nine units has a theme such as animals, plants, exploration, or inventions. The beginning lessons have a text that is about a half page long. The length gradually increases to about a page. The texts in the first unit are purposely easy and cover information the students already know so that with this comparatively easy material, they can get used to the book, the class, and the instructor.

Vocabulary. One of the primary tasks of beginning students is memorizing vocabulary. They usually use their bilingual dictionaries to make a list of new words with their translations. In this book, about ten words are introduced in each lesson. They are in boldface type. Those underlined are illustrated or glossed in the margin. All of the words are used at least five times in the lesson, and then are repeated several more times in later lessons. There is also a context clue exercise at the end of each unit that teaches some of the vocabulary for the following unit.

Students should use their dictionaries only for the meaning of words that are not glossed, illustrated, or obvious from the context. Because the words are used in several different sentences, students learn them without tedious memorization and see how they are used in different contexts. They can test themselves on vocabulary at the end of each lesson by going through the boldface words. The boldface is also useful when the students want to review.

Because vocabulary is introduced gradually and then used repeatedly, the lessons should be done in order. Otherwise students will be confronted with too many new vocabulary items in one lesson.

The vocabulary is all useful for beginning academic students except for a few words such as *kiwi, hyacinth, guayule,* and *bamboo* which are necessary for the text.

Structure. The first two units use only the present tense, and the sentences are short. The past tense is introduced in Unit III and the present continuous in Unit V. The only other tenses used are the past continuous and the future with *will* and *going to*. Subject, object, possessive, and reflexive pronouns are used. The book also includes such connectors as *and, but, so, then, because, or*, and *when*. By using these, the text can include longer sentences that are still easy for the students to read.

Exercises

Vocabulary. The first exercise has sentences taken directly from the text. All new words are included. This is for practice in reading the sentences again and writing the new words.

Vocabulary (new context). This exercise gives further practice with the new words in a different context but with the same meaning.

Vocabulary Review. Vocabulary items are used in subsequent texts and exercises to give additional review. They are fill-ins or matching synonyms and antonyms.

Questions. These comprehension questions are taken directly from the text. They can be done orally in class, and/or the students can write the answers as homework. Those marked with an asterisk are either inference or discussion questions.

Comprehension. These are either true/false, true/false/no information, or multiple choice. There are also inference and discussion questions marked with an asterisk.

Main Idea. Students must choose the main idea of the text from three possibilities.

Word Study. There is a word study section at the end of each unit. It reinforces structural points such as verb forms, pronouns, and comparison of adjectives that the students are learning in other classes. It also gives spelling rules for noun plurals and verb endings. Later units have charts of word forms. Each unit has an exercise on context clues using vocabulary items for the following unit. The exercises are not intended to be complete explanations and practice of the grammar points. The material in this section is included in the quizzes in the instructor's manual.

Teaching Methods

I suggest that the instructor read the text aloud as a pronunciation model, explaining vocabulary so that students don't have to use their bilingual dictionaries.

Then the class can do the exercises, with the instructor writing the answers on the board. For variety, students might do the exercises together in small groups. Then the class as a whole can go over the exercises quickly.

Students need to understand the subject matter so they can answer the comprehension and main idea questions, but they should not be required to learn the information. It should be stressed to the students that the purpose of this text is to teach reading skills and vocabulary, not information. Otherwise, they will be spending hours memorizing facts that they don't need to know. Unit V has one question on the main idea at the end of the unit. Students have to match details from the five lessons with the five titles. I suggest that they do this together in class, since they have not been required to learn the information in the lessons.

The quizzes in the manual test reading skills with a new text related to the ones in the unit. There are comprehension and main idea questions for it.

Since students are not required to learn the information, they can go through the book fairly quickly. It is probably necessary to go through the first unit slowly, but after that I suggest that the students do about one lesson together in class and one as homework each day. The students can do a lesson together in class. The instructor can then read the next text and assign that lesson for homework. The next day he or she can go over the assignment in class, do another lesson, and assign another. Students should read each text two or three times as homework. At the end of each lesson they should test themselves on the boldface vocabulary items and memorize any that they haven't learned through use.

Of course lessons never come out exactly to fit this schedule, but a class should be able to complete the book in an eight-week program with classes that meet every day, or in a semester program where classes meet less frequently.

Students should learn all of the material in the word study sections. It is all basic material that they need to know. The explanations are purposely very simple so that students can understand them. Most instructors will want to give further explanations as they present each part.

There is ample material for class discussions if the text is used in conjunction with a spoken English class. Otherwise, there is no need to discuss the content of the lessons, except to verify comprehension.

There are no timed readings. Students should be allowed to read at their own speed so that they have time to notice everything they possibly can about the English language.

Quizzes

There is a short quiz for Lessons 1 and 2 so that the instructor can test the students during the first week of classes. This quiz includes questions on the lessons on the kiwi and the camel.

All the other quizzes are unit tests. They include a vocabulary question like the first two exercises in the lessons. There is a short reading passage with comprehension and main idea questions. There are also questions on the material in the Word Study sections. Each quiz has 25 to 40 questions. The students should be able to do the quizzes in about 13 to 20 minutes, allowing a half minute for each item.

Unit I

ANIMALS I

THE KIWI

1

The **kiwi** lives **only** in New Zealand. It is a very **strange** bird because it cannot **fly**.

The kiwi is the same **size** as a chicken. It has no **wings** or **tail**. It does not have any **feathers**
5 like other birds. It has hair on its body. Each foot has four toes. Its **beak** (mouth) is very long.

A kiwi likes a lot of trees around it. It sleeps **during** the day because the sunlight **hurts** its eyes. It can **smell** things with its nose. It is the only
10 bird in the world that can smell things. The kiwi's eggs are very big.

There are only a few kiwis in New Zealand now. People never see them. The **government** says that people cannot kill kiwis. New Zealanders
15 want their kiwis to live.

There is a picture of a kiwi on New Zealand money. People from New Zealand are sometimes called kiwis.

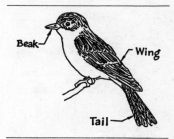

A. Vocabulary

Put the right word in the blanks. The sentences are from the text.

government	smell	during	kiwi
kill	size	fly	only
wings	chicken	beak	tail
strange	hurts	feathers	body

1. It sleeps _____ the day because the sunlight _____ its eyes.
2. It is a very _____ bird because it cannot _____ .
3. The _____ says that people cannot kill kiwis.
4. It can _____ things with its nose.
5. It has no _____ or _____ .
6. The _____ lives _____ in New Zealand.
7. It does not have any _____ like other birds.
8. Its _____ (mouth) is very long.
9. The kiwi is the same _____ as a chicken.

B. Vocabulary (new context)

Put the right word in the blanks. These are new sentences for the same words.

during	pictures	kiwi	only
size	smells	wings	hair
hurts	strange	tail	feathers
trees	government	fly	beak

1. The _____ and a few other birds cannot fly.
2. A bluebird has blue _____ .
3. Some students have a scholarship from their _____ .
4. An airplane can _____ because it has _____ .
5. What are you cooking? It _____ good.
6. My leg _____ . I can't walk on it.
7. Most cats have a long _____ .
8. A person has a mouth. A bird has a _____ .
9. Some students are very _____ . They want to learn English but they don't come to class.

10. I cannot buy this shirt. I have _____ three dollars.
11. What _____ shoes do you wear?
12. Most people work _____ the day and sleep at night.

C. Questions
The asterisk (*) means you have to think of the answer. You cannot find it in the text.

  1. Where does the kiwi live?
  2. What is a kiwi?
  3. How big is a kiwi?
  4. Does a kiwi have feathers?
  5. Does it have a tail and wings?
*6. How many toes does it have?
  7. When does a kiwi sleep?
  8. Can most birds smell?
  9. Why can't people kill kiwis?
*10. Why does the New Zealand government have a picture of a kiwi on its money?

D. Comprehension: True/False
Write **T** if the sentence is true. Write **F** if it is not true. The asterisk (*) means you have to think of the answer. You cannot find it in the text.

_____ 1. Kiwis live in Australia and New Zealand.
_____ 2. A kiwi has a tail but no wings.
_____ 3. A kiwi has a big beak.
_____ 4. It sleeps during the day because light hurts its eyes.
_____ *5. You can see a kiwi in some zoos.
_____ 6. The New Zealand government does not want all the kiwis to die.
_____ 7. A kiwi is like most other birds.

E. Main Idea
Circle the number of the main idea of the text.

1. The kiwi is a strange New Zealand bird.
2. The kiwi sleeps during the day and has no tail or wings.
3. New Zealanders like kiwis.

THE CAMEL

2

The **camel** can go without water for a long time. Some people think it **stores** water in its **hump**. This is not true. It stores food in its hump. The camel's body changes the food into fat. Then it
5 stores the fat in its hump. It cannot store the fat **all over** its body. Fat all over an animal's body keeps the animal warm. Camels live in the **desert**. They do not want to be warm during the day.

keeps

everywhere

The desert is very hot. The camel gets hotter
10 and hotter during the day. It stores this **heat** in its body because the nights are **cool**.

noun for *hot*
a little cold

The Arabian camel has one hump. The Bactrian camel of Central Asia has two humps. It **also** has long **thick** hair because the winters are cold in
15 Central Asia.

too

There is a lot of sand in the desert. The camel has long **eyelashes**. The sand cannot go into the camel's eyes.

Arabic has **about** 150 words to **describe** a
20 camel. Arabs need all these words because the camel is very important to them.

about = more or less / describe = tell about

ANIMALS I

A. Vocabulary
Put the right word in the blanks. The sentences are from the text.

all over	during	eyelashes	hump
also	cool	thick	desert
stores	camel	describe	winters
sand	about	fat	heat

1. Arabic has _____ 150 words to _____ a camel.
2. The _____ can go without water for a long time.
3. The camel has long _____ .
4. Some people think it_____ water in its_____ .
5. Camels live in the _____ .
6. It _____ has long _____ hair because the winters are cold in Central Asia.
7. It cannot store the fat _____ its body.
8. It stores this _____ in its body because the nights are _____ .

B. Vocabulary (new context)
Put the right word in the blanks. These are new sentences for the same words.

also	winters	about	hotter
camels	cool	heat	desert
during	food	all over	describe
hump	eyelashes	thick	store

1. We _____ milk, fruit, and vegetables in the refrigerator.
2. Fall is _____ in Canada. Winter is cold. Winter is _____ cold in the Soviet Union.
3. Can you _____ an elephant? What does it look like?
4. There are different animals _____ the world.
5. Some camels have one _____ and some have two.
6. Some people have long _____ on their eyes.
7. It does not rain very much in the _____ .

8. Mark's engineering textbook is very _____ . It has more than 1000 pages.
9. We cook food with _____ from a stove.
10. Not many Arabs ride on _____ . Now they use cars.
11. Tom is _____ 25 years old. Maybe he is 24 or 27.

C. Questions

1. Where do camels live?
2. What does a camel store in its hump?
3. The camel doesn't store fat all over its body. Why?
4. Why does it store heat during the day?
5. Which camel has one hump? Which has two?
6. Why does a Bactrian camel have long thick hair?
7. Why does a camel need long eyelashes?
8. Why does Arabic have 150 words to describe a camel?

D. Comprehension
Put a circle around the letter of the best answer.

1. The camel can go without _____ for a long time.
   a. food
   b. water
   c. fat
   d. heat

2. It stores _____ in its hump.
   a. water
   b. heat
   c. food
   d. hair

3. The _____ camel has one hump.
   a. Arabian
   b. Bactrian

4. Long _____ keep sand out of the camel's eyes.
   a. thick hair
   b. humps
   c. eyelashes
   d. ears

5. The Bactrian camel has long thick hair because _____ .
    a. it lives in a hot desert   c. winters are cold in Central Asia
    b. it stores fat in its hump   d. the sand gets in its eyes

E. Main Idea
Circle the number of the main idea of the text.

1. There are two kinds of camels.
2. The camel has a good body for life in the desert.
3. The camel stores food in its hump.

THE POLAR BEAR

3

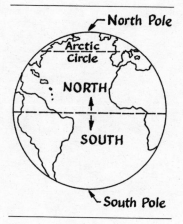

The **polar bear** is a very big white bear. We call it the polar bear because it lives inside the Arctic Circle near the **North** Pole. There are no polar bears at the **South** Pole.

5 The polar bear lives in the **snow** and **ice**. At the North Pole there is only snow, ice, and water. There is not any land. You cannot see the polar bear in the snow because its coat is yellow-white. It has a very **warm** coat because the weather is cold
10 north of the Arctic Circle.

This bear is 3 meters long and it **weighs** 450 kilos. It can stand up on its back legs because it has very **wide** feet. It can use its front legs like arms. The polar bear can **swim** very well. It can swim 120
15 kilometers out into the water. It **catches** fish and sea animals for food. It goes into the sea when it is **afraid**.

People like to kill the polar bear for its beautiful white coat. The governments of Canada,
20 the United States, and the Soviet Union say that no one can kill polar bears now. They do not want all of these beautiful animals to die.

ANIMALS I

A. Vocabulary
Put the right word in the sentences. The sentences are from the text.

polar	South	North	warm
kilos	catches	land	weighs
wide	sea	afraid	inside
bear	snow	swim	ice

1. The polar bear lives in the _____ and _____ .
2. The polar _____ is a very big white bear.
3. It goes into the sea when it is _____ .
4. It has a very _____ coat because the weather is cold north of the Arctic Circle.
5. There are no polar bears at the _____ Pole.
6. The polar bear can _____ very well.
7. We call it the polar bear because it lives inside the Arctic Circle near the _____ Pole.
8. It _____ fish and sea animals for food.
9. This bear is 3 meters long, and it _____ 450 kilos.
10. It can stand up on its back legs because it has very _____ feet.

B. Vocabulary (new context)
Put the right word in the blanks. These are new sentences for the same words.

swim	afraid	North	South
warm	weigh	ice	wide
snow	coat	bears	catch

1. There are brown and black _____ in North America.
2. How much do you _____ ? Fifty kilos?
3. Winter is cold. Spring is _____ . Fall is cool.
4. Sometimes children are _____ of animals.
5. Do you like to _____ in a swimming pool?
6. Italy is _____ of France.
7. There is _____ all over Canada in the winter.
8. Do you want some _____ in your Coke?

9. The Sahara Desert is in _____ Africa.
10. Tenth Street is a _____ street. A lot of cars can go on it at the same time.
11. Can you _____ the ball?

C. Vocabulary Review
Put **C** before the words about camels. Put **K** before the words about kiwis. Some of the words are not about camels or kiwis.

stores heat in its body	eyelashes
hump	beak
tail	desert
big eggs	wing
goes without water	hair on its body
long thick hair	feather

D. Questions
The asterisk (*) means you have to think of the answer.

1. Why do we call this bear the polar bear?
2. Why can't people see the polar bear very well?
3. Why does it have a warm coat?
4. How much does it weigh?
5. What does it eat?
6. Where does it go when it is afraid?
7. Why do people like to kill the polar bear?
8. What do the governments of the Soviet Union, the United States, and Canada say?
*9. Can a polar bear live near New Zealand?
*10. Why doesn't a polar bear eat fruit or vegetables?

E. Comprehension

1. The polar bear lives _____ .
   a. at the South Pole
   b. in warm countries
   c. near the North Pole
   d. on land

2. At the North Pole there is no _____ .
   a. ice
   b. water
   c. snow
   d. land

3. You cannot see the polar bear in the snow because _____ .
   a. it has a yellow-white coat
   b. it goes under the snow
   c. it can run very fast
   d. it goes into the water

4. The polar bear _____ for food.
   a. catches land animals
   b. looks for trees
   c. catches sea animals and fish
   d. looks for fruit and vegetables

5. When the polar bear is afraid, it _____ .
   a. goes into the sea
   b. goes under the snow
   c. runs away
   d. stands up on its wide feet

6. The governments of the Soviet Union, Canada, and the United States say that
   _____ .
   a. the polar bear is beautiful
   b. it has a warm coat
   c. no one can kill the polar bear
   d. it cannot live near the North Pole

F. Main Idea

1. People like to kill polar bears because they have beautiful warm yellow-white coats.
2. Polar bears live inside the Arctic Circle in the snow and ice.
3. Polar bears live inside the Arctic Circle, eat fish and sea animals, and have warm yellow-white coats.

THE HIPPOPOTAMUS 4

The hippopotamus lives in the hot part of Africa. It is a **mammal**. That is, its babies are born **alive**, and they drink milk from the mother's body.

The hippopotamus is a <u>**large**</u> animal. It
5 weighs four tons. Its <u>**stomach**</u> is 7 meters long, but the hippopotamus eats only **plants**. It is a mammal but it **spends** a lot of time in the water.

big

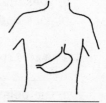

During the day it sleeps <u>**beside**</u> a river or a <u>**lake**</u>. Sometimes it wakes up. Then it goes under
10 the water to get some plants for food. It can close its nose and **stay** under water for ten minutes. Its ears, eyes, and nose are **high** up on its head. It can stay with its body under the water and only its ears, eyes, and nose <u>**above**</u> the water. Then it can
15 **breathe** the air.

at the side of

over

At night the hippo walks on the land and looks for food. It never goes very far from the water.

A baby hippo often stands on its mother's back. The mother looks for food underwater. The
20 baby rides on her back above the water.

A. Vocabulary

stomach	stay	beside	mammal
breathe	lake	plants	spends
above	alive	large	high

1. The hippopotamus is a _____ animal.
2. During the day it sleeps_____ a river or a_____ .
3. It is a _____ .
4. Its _____ is 7 meters long, but the hippopotamus eats only _____ .
5. It can close its nose and _____ under water for 10 minutes.
6. It can stay with its body under the water and only its ears, eyes, and nose _____ the water.
7. Then it can _____ the air.
8. It is a mammal, but it _____ a lot of time in the water.
9. Its eyes, ears, and nose are _____ up on its head.

B. Vocabulary (new context)

beside	Lake	mammal	stomach
plants	stays	breathe	nose
large	above	spend	high

1. The camel is a _____ but the kiwi is a bird.
2. Food goes from your mouth into your _____ .
3. How do you smell a beautiful flower? You _____ in with your nose.
4. Camels eat _____ . Polar bears and kiwis eat meat.
5. I want to talk to you. Please sit _____ me.
6. Tom likes to _____ his free time in the Student Union. He _____ there a few hours every day.
7. Birds can fly _____ the trees.
8. _____ Geneva is a beautiful lake in Switzerland.
9. The polar bear is a _____ animal. It is very big.
10. New York has a lot of _____ buildings.

C. Vocabulary Review
Put a circle around the letter of the best answer.

1. Can you _____ a polar bear? What does it look like?
   a. hurt   c. catch
   b. describe   d. store

2. Many birds fly _____ in the winter to a warmer place.
   a. north   c. south
   b. wing   d. wide

3. These birds fly _____ in the summer to a cooler place.
   a. north   c. south
   b. wing   d. wide

4. Roses _____ beautiful.
   a. swim   c. smell
   b. catch   d. hurt

5. The kiwi is a _____ bird.
   a. strange   c. hurt
   b. warm   d. wide

6. My hand _____ . I can't write.
   a. flies   c. smells
   b. catches   d. hurts

D. Questions

1. Where does the hippopotamus live?
*2. Is a kiwi a mammal?
3. How long is a hippo's stomach?
4. Does a hippo eat meat?
5. Why does a hippo go under water?
6. How can it stay under water for 10 minutes?
*7. Can it breathe under water? Why?
8. What does it do at night?
9. Where does a baby hippo ride?
*10. Is a bear a mammal?

E. Comprehension: True/False/No Information

Put **T** if the sentence is true. Put **F** if it is false. Put **NI** if there is no information about the sentence.

_____ 1. Hippo babies are born alive.

_____ 2. Birds and hippos eat plants.

_____ 3. Hippos live under water.

_____ 4. A hippo can close its eyes.

_____ 5. A hippo breathes under water.

_____ 6. A hippo looks for food on the land during the day.

_____ 7. A hippo has long eyelashes to keep water out of its eyes.

F. Main Idea

1. The hippopotamus is a large African animal that spends a lot of time in the water and eats plants.
2. The hippopotamus has eyes, ears, and nose high up on its head.
3. The hippopotamus walks on the land at night, and it eats and sleeps during the day.

THE DOLPHIN

5

Can **dolphins** talk? Maybe they can't talk
with words, but they talk with **sounds**. They **show**
their feelings with sounds.

Dolphins **travel** in a **group**. We call a group
5 of fish a "school." Dolphins don't study, but they
travel **together**. Dolphins are mammals, not fish,
but they swim together in a school.

Dolphins talk to the other dolphins in the
school. They give information. They tell when they
10 are happy or sad or afraid. They say "Welcome"
when a dolphin comes back to the school. They talk
when they play.

They make a few sounds above water. They
make many more sounds underwater. People can-
15 not hear these sounds because they are very, very
high. **Scientists** make tapes of the sounds and
study them.

Sometimes people catch a dolphin for a large
aquarium. (An aquarium is a zoo for fish.) People
20 can watch the dolphins in a show. Dolphins don't
like to be away from their school in an aquarium.
They are sad and **lonely**.

There are many stories about dolphins. Dolphins help people. Sometimes they **save** some-
25 body's life. Dolphin meat is good, but people don't
like to kill dolphins. People say that dolphins bring
good luck. Many people **believe** this.

ANIMALS I

A. Vocabulary

together	mammals	travel	believe
dolphins	lonely	group	aquarium
save	show	sounds	scientists

1. Dolphins _____ in a _____ .
2. Sometimes they _____ somebody's life.
3. Can _____ talk?
4. Sometimes people catch a dolphin for a large _____ .
5. They are sad and _____ .
6. They _____ their feelings with sounds.
7. _____ make tapes of their sounds and study them.
8. Many people _____ this.
9. Dolphins don't study, but they travel _____ .
10. Maybe they can't talk with words, but they talk with _____ .

B. Vocabulary (new context)

lonely	dolphin	together	save
sounds	believe	scientists	aquarium
show	travel	feelings	group

1. The _____ is a mammal but it lives in the sea.
2. Many students at a large university feel _____ . They don't have many friends.
3. Do you like to _____ to different countries?
4. Please _____ me your composition.
5. Children like to play _____ in the snow.
6. There is a _____ of Omani students in our class.
7. Is it true? Do you _____ it?
8. _____ study animals and many other things.
9. There are many interesting fish and sea animals at an _____ .
10. You must _____ your money. Don't spend it on a new car.
11. It is difficult to pronounce some English _____ .

C. Vocabulary Review
Put these words under the right titles. Some words go under more than one title.

1. Parts of an Animal's Body   **2. Parts of a Person's Body**

eyelashes	hump	wing	feather
tail	beak	nose	arm
leg	stomach	hand	eyes

D. Questions

1. Can dolphins talk?
2. What is a school of dolphins?
3. What do dolphins talk about?
4. When do they say "Welcome"?
5. Do they make more sounds above or underwater?
6. Can people hear dolphin sounds? Why?
7. How does a dolphin feel in an aquarium?
*8. Do dolphins bring good luck?
*9. Dolphins are not fish. What is the difference between dolphins and fish?

E. Comprehension

1. Dolphins talk with _____ .
   a. words   c. sounds
   b. their hands   d. music

2. Dolphins talk when they _____ .
   a. play   c. show
   b. listen   d. kill

3. They make more sounds _____ .
   a. above water   c. for tapes
   b. underwater   d. in school

4. Scientists study _____ of dolphins.
   a. shows
   b. schools
   c. aquariums
   d. tapes

5. Dolphins like to be _____ .
   a. at an aquarium
   b. in their school
   c. lonely
   d. on tapes

6. What sentence is *not* true?
   a. A dolphin can save a person's life.
   b. People like to watch dolphins.
   c. Dolphins always bring good luck.
   d. A dolphin can talk with sounds.

F. Main Idea

1. Dolphins use words to show how they feel and to give information.
2. Dolphins travel together and talk with sounds.
3. Dolphins live in the sea and in aquariums.
4. The dolphin is a mammal, and scientists can tape it.

WORD STUDY

A. Possessive Pronouns

These pronouns show that something belongs to somebody.

Example: **My** car is new.
            Their hair is thick.

singular	plural
I – my	we – our
you – your	you – your
she – her	they – their
he – his	
it – its	

Put the right pronoun in the blanks.

1. The camel stores food in _____ hump.
2. Maria likes _____ classes this year.
3. I use _____ dictionary every day.
4. Polar bears use _____ front legs like arms.
5. Do you have _____ cassette tapes with you?
6. Scientists listen to _____ tapes.
7. Carlos and his family swim in _____ pool every day.
8. David drives _____ car to class.
9. We go to the university on _____ bicycles.
10. A baby hippo rides on _____ mother's back.

B. Verbs—Present Tense

Put an **s** on the simple verb for the present tense. Do not put an s with **I, you, we** or **they**.

a dolphin	plays	I	play
a girl	plays	you	play
a man	plays	we	play
she	plays	they	play
he	plays		
it	plays		

C. Spelling

1. When a simple verb ends in **y** with a consonant before it, change the **y** to **i** and add **-es**.

        fly – flies   study – studies

2. When a simple verb ends in **y** with a vowel before it, add **-s**.

        play – plays   say – says

3. When a simple verb ends in **s, ch, sh, x,** or **z,** add **-es**.

        catch – catches   finish – finishes

4. Irregular:

        go – goes   do – does   have – has
        be – am, is, are

Change each sentence and make a new one. Use the word in parentheses. You must change some pronouns too.

Example: (I)   They study every day.
                I study every day.

(a polar bear)   1. We catch fish and eat them.
(they)   2. Mike usually flies home.
(I)   3. Betty has a beautiful plant in her living room.
(people)   4. David likes dolphin shows.
(we)   5. They travel only in the summer.
(a dolphin)   6. You play in the water.
(they)   7. We go swimming in a lake in summer.
(Tom)   8. I usually finish my work early.
(a mammal)   9. People are born alive.
(Ann and Bill) 10. Ali does his homework in the afternoon.

D. Comparisons

Sometimes we compare two things. We tell how they are different. Add **-er** to short words (words with only one syllable) to compare two things. Use **than**.

Example: A camel is big. A polar bear is **bigger than** a camel.
            Carlos is twenty years old. David is eighteen. Carlos is **older than**
               David.

Spelling: When a word has **one** syllable with **one** vowel in the middle and **one** consonant at the end, double the consonant and add **-er**. This is the one-one-one (1-1-1) rule.

Example: big – bigger   hot – hotter

Put the right comparison form in the sentence.

(strange)   1. A kiwi is _____ a bluebird.
(thick)   2. A Bactrian camel's hair is _____ an Arabian camel's hair.
(hot)   3. Oman is _____ Switzerland.
(warm)   4. Italy is _____ France.
(large)   5. Saudi Arabia is _____ Kuwait.
(tall)   6. Marie is _____ Masako.
(fat)   7. John is _____ than Robert.
(young)   8. My sister is _____ my brother.
(cold)   9. Ice is _____ water.
(small)   10. A dolphin is _____ a polar bear.

E. Context Clues

Sometimes you can understand a new word from the other words in the sentence. Read each sentence. Then choose the meaning of the new word. **Do not use your dictionary.** These are new words for the next unit.

1. A cat can **climb** a tree. A camel cannot.
   a. sit under   c. walk near
   b. go up   d. fly into

2. Fish live in lakes, rivers, and **oceans**.
   a. seas   c. trees
   b. north   d. south

3. Queen Elizabeth II is a very **famous** woman.
   a. everyone likes her
   b. everyone studies about her in English class
   c. everyone knows about her
   d. everyone talks to her

4. It is easy to make a salad. **Mix** some lettuce, tomatoes, and cucumber.
   a. put together
   b. eat
   c. take out of the refrigerator
   d. buy

5. Indonesia, the Philippines, Senegal, and Cuba are in the **tropics**.
   a. hot, dry countries
   b. cold, dry countries
   c. cold, wet countries
   d. hot, wet countries

6. Paul **enjoys** sports. He plays soccer and basketball. He watches sports on television.
   a. looks at
   b. likes
   c. plays
   d. watches

7. A Ping-Pong ball is **small**. A basketball is large.
   a. old
   b. little
   c. new
   d. big

8. A polar bear runs **toward** the sea when it is afraid.
   a. from
   b. in
   c. to
   d. of

9. Mrs. Mora **feeds** her birds every day.
   a. washes
   b. breathes
   c. saves
   d. gives food to

10. **Both** Isamu and Kumiko are from Japan.
    a. the two of them
    b. not any
    c. the five of them
    d. all of them

11. This is a **difficult** problem: 7,958,395 ÷ 9687.
    a. not easy
    b. thick
    c. easy
    d. cool

12. Mr. Baker is 75 years old **so** he can't play baseball.
    a. He likes to play baseball.
    b. He doesn't want to play baseball.
    c. He plays baseball every day.
    d. He can't play baseball because he is 75 years old.

13. Mr. Baker is 75. He can't hear sounds very well. He is **deaf**.
    a. can't see   c. can't hear
    b. can't walk   d. can't run

14. Tom wants a **whole** sandwich. I want only half of a sandwich.
    a. all of it   c. some of it
    b. part of it   d. 1/4 of it

Unit
II

HOW? WHY?

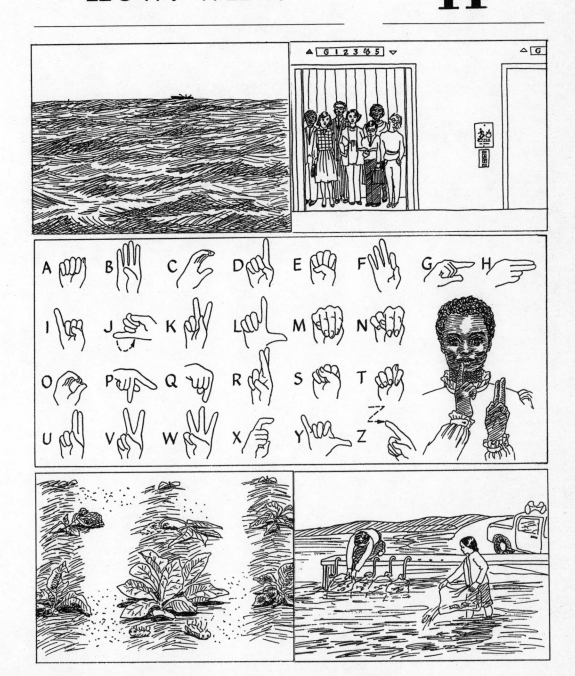

WHY ARE ELEVATORS IMPORTANT?

1

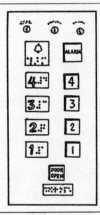

An **elevator** is **wonderful.** It is **really** only a small room. Rooms usually stay in one place. Elevators travel up and down all day long.

Sometimes a worker stands in the elevator.
5   He or she runs it up and down. In **modern** elevators there is no worker. The people walk in. They know what floors they want. They push a **button** and the elevator goes to that floor. It is all very fast and easy.

10   Elevators are very important to us. Why? Think about a tall building. Maybe it has twenty floors. Maybe it has fifty or more. Who can walk up all those **stairs**? Maybe people can **climb** them one time. Can someone climb thirty floors to an
15   office every day? Can small children walk up to their apartments on the twenty-fourth floor? Can their mother and father **carry** food up all those stairs? Of course not.

We can have high buildings because we have
20   elevators. We **could** not have all the beautiful tall buildings in the world without elevators. They are really wonderful.

??????????

A. Vocabulary

worker	stairs	apartment	elevator
button	wonderful	modern	carry
really	climb	office	could

1. Who can walk up all those _____?
2. An _____ is _____.
3. Can their mother and father _____ food up all those stairs?
4. It is _____ only a small room.
5. Maybe people can _____ them one time.
6. They push a _____ and the elevator goes to that floor.
7. In _____ elevators there is no worker.
8. We _____ not have all the beautiful tall buildings in the world without elevators.

B. Vocabulary (new context)

stairs	modern	could	elevator
really	floor	worker	climb
buttons	wonderful	carry	push

1. Tokyo has a lot of high buildings. It is a _____ city.
2. You usually breathe hard when you walk up a lot of _____.
3. A group of people can ride together in an _____.
4. A bus can _____ a lot of people at one time.
5. Dolphins cannot _____ talk. They use sounds, not words.
6. Modern telephones have the numbers on _____.
7. Cats like to _____ trees.
8. Children think that a zoo is a _____ place to visit.
9. _____ you please help me for a minute?

C. Vocabulary Review

breathe	describe	beside	sound
group	together	believe	save
scientists	show	aquarium	lonely
during	store	all over	cooler

1. Can you _____ an aquarium? Tell me about one.
2. Some _____ teach at universities and some work in laboratories.
3. There are two small tables _____ the sofa.
4. There are beautiful plants _____ the park.
5. Don't walk to class every day. Buy a bicycle. You can _____ time.
6. I don't _____ you. It isn't true.
7. Keiko is _____ . She wants to see her friends and family.
8. Maria and Tony usually study _____ .
9. An _____ is an interesting place to visit.
10. It is _____ under a tree than in the sun.

D. Questions

1. What is an elevator really?
2. How is an elevator different from other rooms?
3. Does a worker run a modern elevator?
4. How do people make an elevator go up and down?
5. Can people walk up twenty or forty floors every day?
6. Why can we have high buildings?

E. Comprehension

1. An elevator is a small _____ .
   a. room
   b. building
   c. stairs
   d. button

2. In modern elevators there is no _____ .
   a. button
   b. light
   c. worker
   d. travel

3. An elevator travels _____ .
   a. inside and outside
   b. in and out
   c. under and above
   d. up and down

4. People _____ climb thirty floors every day.
   a. like to
   b. cannot
   c. can
   d. want to

5. We have _____ because we have elevators.
   a. high buildings
   b. new cars
   c. old buses
   d. wide streets

F. Main Idea

1. People cannot climb a lot of floors in a tall building.
2. We can have high buildings because we have elevators.
3. An elevator is a small room.

WHY IS THE SEA SALTY?

2

There is a lot of **salt** on the **earth,** and it **mixes** very well with water.

There is some salt in all water. Water on the land runs into lakes and rivers. These rivers run
5 into the seas and **oceans**. They carry a little salt with them. Some of the ocean water **moves** into the air and **clouds**. It **evaporates**. Salt cannot evaporate. It stays in the ocean.

The water in the oceans has more salt than
10 river water. Ocean water is about 3-1/2% (three and a half **percent**) salt. Some seas have more salt than others.

Some lakes do not have a river to carry the water and salt away. Some of the water **leaves** the
15 lakes. It evaporates, but the salt cannot. These lakes are very salty. There are two **famous** lakes like this. They are the Dead Sea in the Middle East and Great Salt Lake in the state of Utah in the United States. They are much saltier than the
20 Atlantic Ocean and the Pacific Ocean.

world

seas

goes away from

??????????

A. Vocabulary

evaporates	salt	leaves	percent
stays	moves	clouds	land
oceans	earth	mixes	famous

1. Ocean water is about three and a half _____ salt.
2. There is a lot of _____ on the _____ , and it _____ very well with the water.
3. Some of the water _____ the lakes.
4. There are two _____ lakes like this.
5. These rivers run into the seas and _____ .
6. Some of the ocean water _____ into the air and _____ .
7. It _____ .

B. Vocabulary (new context)

evaporates	earth	percent	ocean
salt	state	earth	mix
clouds	others	water	famous
moves	river	leave	

1. Two of the students have to _____ the class early.
2. The _____ is round. It _____ around the sun.
3. Most people put _____ on their food.
4. Muhammad Ali was a _____ boxer.
5. Some people put sugar in their coffee. Then they _____ it with a spoon.
6. Some of the water in a swimming pool _____ .
7. The Pacific _____ is bigger than the Atlantic Ocean.
8. There are beautiful white _____ in the sky today.
9. Eighty _____ of the class are men.

??????????

C. Vocabulary Review

Underline the word that does not belong with the other two.

Example: red, <u>book</u>, blue

1. zoo, aquarium, university
2. lake, snow, ice
3. elevator, stairs, car
4. together, modern, new
5. polar bear, dolphin, kiwi
6. carry, climb, walk up
7. cool, warm, thick
8. scientist, teacher, saltier

D. Questions

1. What does salt mix well with?
2. Is there salt in lakes and rivers?
3. Where does river water go?
4. Where does some of the ocean water go?
5. Where does the salt in the ocean go?
6. Which has more salt, rivers or oceans?
7. Why are some lakes very salty?
8. Name two famous salty lakes.
9. What is Utah? Where is it?
10. Which is saltier, the Atlantic Ocean or the Dead Sea?
*11. Are there fish in the Dead Sea?

E. Comprehension: True/False

_____   1. Salt mixes with water.
_____   *2. Clouds have salt in them.
_____   3. Water on the land moves into lakes and rivers.
_____   4. There is salt in rivers.
_____   5. Rivers have more salt than oceans.
_____   6. Salt evaporates.
_____   7. Ocean water is about 2-1/4% salt.
_____   *8. Water leaves some lakes only in rivers.
_____   9. Great Salt Lake is in the United States.

??????????

F. Main Idea

1. The sea is salty because water evaporates and salt doesn't.
2. The sea is salty because rivers run into oceans.
3. Water moves from the land to rivers to oceans to clouds and to the land again.

HOW CAN A PLANT KILL?

3

People **kill**. Animals kill. Animals and people kill for food or they kill their **enemies**. People and animals can move around and find something to kill. They can run away from an enemy. They can
5 kill it **if** it is necessary.

enemies ≠ friends

Many **kinds** of animals eat plants. The plants cannot run away from their enemies. Some plants make **poison**. If an animal eats part of the plant, it gets sick or dies. Animals learn to stay away from
10 these plants. There are many kinds of plants that make poison. Most of them **grow** in the desert or in the **tropics**.

hot, wet countries

Today **farmers** use many kinds of poison on their **farms**. Most of these poisons come from
15 petroleum, but petroleum is **expensive**. Scientists **collect** poisonous plants and study them. Maybe farmers can use **cheap** poison from plants **instead of** expensive poison from petroleum.

costs a lot

cheap ≠ expensive

??????????

A. Vocabulary

kill	tropics	farmers	instead of
enemies	scientists	poison	cheap
plant	if	grow	farms
kinds	run away	collect	expensive

1. Many _____ of animals eat plants.
2. Animals and people kill for food or they kill their _____ .
3. Today _____ use many kinds of poison on their _____ .
4. Scientists _____ poisonous plants and study them.
5. Some plants make _____ .
6. Maybe farmers can use _____ poison from plants _____ expensive poison from petroleum.
7. Most of them _____ in the desert or in the _____ .
8. They can kill it _____ it is necessary.
9. Most of these poisons come from petroleum, but petroleum is _____ .

B. Vocabulary (new context)

expensive	tropics	petroleum	grow
cheap	scientist	collect	if
instead of	farm	kind	kill
most	farmers	poison	enemies

1. David's family has a big _____ . His family are _____ .
2. A Mercedes Benz is an _____ car.
3. Please come to the Student Union at 12:00 _____ you can.
4. Malaysia, Togo, and Nigeria are in the _____ .
5. Please write the answers on paper _____ in the book.
6. Ali, please _____ all the students' papers.
7. Some things we use in the garden are _____ . We must keep them away from children.
8. People are the only _____ of polar bears.

9. What _____ of car do you have?
10. _____ clothes are not usually very good.
11. Children _____ very fast. They need new clothes every few months.

C. Vocabulary Review

Find a word or words in Column B that mean the same as a word in Column A. Write the letter and word from Column B beside the word from Column A. The first one is done for you.

Column A

1. earth _____d. world_____
2. ocean _____
3. large _____
4. climb _____
5. percent _____
6. together _____
7. warm _____
8. cool _____
9. leave _____
10. modern _____
11. breathe _____

Column B

a. go
b. %
c. new
d. world
e. go up
f. take air into the body
g. a little hot
h. sea
i. button
j. big
k. lonely
l. a little cold
m. in a group

D. Questions

1. Why do people and animals kill?
2. Can plants run away from an enemy?
3. What do some plants make?
4. What happens to an animal that eats this poison?
5. What do animals learn about these plants?
6. Where do most poisonous plants grow?
*7. Why do farmers use poison on their farms?
8. Where do most poisons come from?
9. Why do scientists collect and study poisonous plants?

??????????

E. Comprehension

1. Animals and people kill their _____ .
   a. poisons
   b. enemies
   c. plants
   d. farmers

2. _____ cannot move around.
   a. Plants
   b. Animals
   c. Farmers
   d. Scientists

3. An animal _____ if it eats a poisonous plant.
   a. gets sick or dies
   b. runs away
   c. moves around
   d. studies the poison

4. Most poisonous plants grow in the desert or in the _____ .
   a. farms
   b. tropics
   c. Arctic Circle
   d. laboratories

5. _____ use many kinds of poisons.
   a. Scientists
   b. Workers
   c. Farmers
   d. Animals

6. Most of these poisons come from _____ .
   a. plants
   b. deserts
   c. petroleum
   d. the tropics

7. Scientists _____ poisonous plants.
   a. use
   b. run away from
   c. buy
   d. collect

8. Poison from plants is _____ than poison from petroleum.
   a. cheaper
   b. more afraid
   c. more expensive
   d. cooler

F. Main Idea

1. Some plants make poisons, and maybe farmers can use them.
2. Plants make poison because they cannot run away from their enemies.
3. Scientists study poisonous plants because farmers want to use them.

HOW CAN WE HAVE FARMS IN THE SEA?

4

Farmers grow plants and animals on their farms. Is it also **possible** to have a farm in the sea?

People in many countries grow **fresh water** fish from eggs. They move the small fish into lakes 5 and rivers. The fish live and grow there. People go fishing in these lakes and rivers. They **enjoy** catching fish. Fish is also good food.

not salty

like

Now Japan grows salt water fish. Most of them are yellowtail fish. Workers grow the fish 10 from eggs. Every time they **feed** the fish, they play tapes of **piano music**. The fish learn that piano music means food.

give food to

When the fish are **small**, the Japanese put them in the ocean near the land. The fish find some 15 of their **own** food. Workers also feed them. They play the same piano music. The fish **already** know this music. They swim **toward** it and find the food. In a few months the fish are large. The Japanese play the same music. The fish swim toward it and 20 the workers catch them.

little

to

The Japanese get about 15 percent of their seafood from farms in the ocean.

??????????

A. Vocabulary

music	piano	fresh	possible
seafood	small	toward	lakes
already	own	feed	enjoy

1. When the fish are _____ , the Japanese put them in the ocean near the land.
2. Is it also _____ to have a farm in the sea?
3. The fish _____ know this music.
4. They swim _____ it.
5. People in many countries grow _____ water fish from eggs.
6. They _____ catching fish.
7. Every time they _____ the fish, they play tapes of _____ _____ .
8. The fish find some of their _____ food.

B. Vocabulary (new context)

feed	small	possible	toward
near	fresh	music	own
enjoy	swim	already	piano

1. The Honda is a _____ car.
2. We cannot drink sea water. We drink _____ water.
3. You _____ know a lot of English words.
4. Rivers run _____ the sea.
5. Is it _____ to travel to the moon?
6. Do you _____ snow and cold weather?
7. Can you play the _____ ?
8. Do you enjoy listening to _____ ?
9. Babies cannot cook their own food. We have to _____ them.
10. Do you ride to class with a friend or do you have your _____ car?

C. Vocabulary Review

Match each word in Column A with its opposite word in Column B. Write the letter and word from Column B next to the word in Column A. The first answer is done for you.

Column A

1. cool ___d. warm___
2. black _____
3. north _____
4. cannot _____
5. travel _____
6. false _____
7. old _____
8. leave _____
9. spend _____
10. under _____

Column B

a. white
b. true
c. modern
d. warm
e. stay home
f. cloud
g. save
h. mix
i. south
j. stay
k. can
l. above

D. Questions

1. Is it possible to have a farm in the ocean?
2. Why do people grow fresh water fish?
3. What country grows salt water fish?
4. What do the Japanese do when they feed the fish?
5. What do the fish learn?
6. When do the workers put the fish in the ocean?
7. When do the workers play the same piano music?
8. Why do the fish swim toward this music?
9. Why do the workers play music when the fish are large?
10. How much food does Japan get from fish farms in the ocean?
*11. Do these fish like piano music? Why?
*12. Why are fish farms important to the world?

E. Comprehension: True/False

_____   1. People can grow fresh water and salt water fish.
_____   2. The Japanese move the fish into the sea when they are large.
_____   3. Piano music means food to most people.
_____   *4. Fish and birds grow from eggs.
_____   5. All fish think that piano music means food.
_____   6. The Japanese use piano music to catch fish.
_____   7. Fish on ocean farms find some of their own food.
_____   8. The Japanese grow about 5 percent of their salt water fish on farms.

F. Main Idea

1. The Japanese use piano music on their salt water farms.
2. It is possible to grow fresh water fish and salt water fish on farms.
3. The Japanese get about 15 percent of their seafood from farms.

HOW DO DEAF PEOPLE TALK?

5

Deaf people cannot hear sounds. How do they "hear" words and talk?

Deaf people use American **Sign** Language (ASL). They talk with their hands. Sometimes two
5 deaf people talk to **each other**. They **both** use ASL. Sometimes a person who can hear **interprets** for deaf people. The person listens to someone talking, and then he or she makes hand signs.

10 There are two kinds of sign language. One kind has a sign for every letter in the alphabet. The person spells every word. This is finger spelling. The other kind has a sign for every word. There are about 5,000 of these signs. They are signs for
15 verbs, things and **ideas**.

Some of the signs are very easy, for example, eat, milk, and house. You can see what they mean. Others are more **difficult**, for example, **star**, egg, or week.

20 People from any country can learn ASL. They use signs, not words, **so** they can understand people from other countries.

ASL is almost like a **dance**. The **whole** body talks. American Sign Language is a beautiful
25 language.

two of them

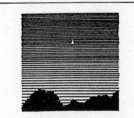

all of it

??????????

A. Vocabulary

ideas	deaf	difficult	star
each other	example	interprets	both
so	whole	sign	dance

1. Others are more _____ , for example, _____ , egg, or week.
2. Sometimes two deaf people talk to _____ .
3. They _____ use ASL.
4. _____ people cannot hear sounds.
5. ASL is almost like a _____ .
6. The _____ body talks.
7. Sometimes a person who can hear _____ for deaf people.
8. They use signs, not words, _____ they can understand people from other countries.
9. Deaf people use American _____ Language.
10. They are signs for verbs, things, and _____ .

B. Vocabulary (new context)

difficult	so	finger	dance
deaf	each other	idea	stars
sign	interprets	both	whole

1. The class wants to have a party. This is a good _____ .
2. Mary cannot hear anything. She is _____ .
3. Ali works for the government. He _____ Arabic and English.
4. A large _____ says "No Smoking."
5. Masako and Carlos speak English to _____ .
6. Nadia and David _____ study engineering.
7. You cannot see the _____ in the sky during the daytime.
8. Japanese is a _____ language. English is easy.
9. It is late _____ we cannot study any more.
10. The _____ class is here today. Everyone is here.
11. There is a _____ for foreign students on Saturday.

??????????

C. Vocabulary Review

evaporates	famous	clouds	enemies
kind	expensive	if	cheaper
poison	collect	tropics	instead of
possible	music	already	enjoy

1. There are a lot of _____ in the sky today. It is cloudy.
2. Dogs and cats are _____ .
3. Michael Jackson is a _____ singer.
4. The weather is hot and wet in the _____ .
5. Do you _____ movies?
6. What _____ of bicycle do you have?
7. Please tell me _____ I talk too fast.
8. Water _____ into the air.
9. It is 8:58 and the students are _____ in their seats for their nine o'clock class.
10. Are apartments _____ or cheap in your city?
11. A bicycle is _____ than a car.
12. Some students listen to _____ when they study.

D. Questions

1. How do deaf people "talk"?
2. How does a person interpret for deaf people?
*3. How many signs are there for finger spelling?
4. How many word signs are there?
5. Why are some signs easy?
6. Why can people from different countries talk to each other with ASL?
7. Why is ASL almost like a dance?
*8. Why is ASL a beautiful language?

E. Comprehension: True/False/No Information

_____ 1. Deaf people cannot hear sounds.
_____ 2. A person who interprets for deaf people cannot hear.
_____ 3. There are more signs for words than for letters.
_____ 4. Japanese use ASL.
_____ 5. Finger spelling has signs for numbers.
_____ 6. Africans cannot learn ASL because they don't speak English.
_____ 7. Only the hands move in ASL.
_____ 8. It is difficult for children to learn ASL.

F. Main Idea

1. ASL helps deaf people talk, but it is difficult to learn.
2. There are two kinds of sign language.
3. ASL is a beautiful language that helps deaf people talk to others.

WORD STUDY

A. Questions: Present Tense

be: Put **be** before the complete subject.

	subject	verb	
Example:	**Fish**	**are**	animals.
	Are fish		animals?

other verbs: Put **do/does** at the beginning of the sentence. Use the simple verb.

	subject	verb	
Example:	**Workers**	**move**	the fish into the sea.
	Do workers	**move**	the fish into the sea?

A worker moves the fish.
Does a worker move   the fish?

Change each sentence to a question.

1. A large house is expensive.
2. Bill does his homework in the afternoon.
3. Rivers run toward the ocean.
4. People drink fresh water.
5. Mary is a good tennis player.
6. Helen feeds her cat every morning.
7. David has his own car.
8. An elevator goes up and down.
9. Kiwis are strange birds.
10. I am late.

B. There is/there are

Use **There is** before a singular noun. Then use **it**.

Example: **There is an elevator** in our apartment building. **It** is
near the stairs.

Use **There are** before a plural noun. Then use **they**.

Example: **There are farms** in the sea. **They** are in Japan.

Look at the noun after the blank. Then write **There is** or **There are** in the first blank. Write **it** or **they** in the second blank.

1. _____ a kiwi in our zoo. _____ sleeps during the day.
2. _____ two black bears also. _____ come from Canada.
3. _____ a chair beside the window. _____ is blue.
4. _____ wonderful mountains in India. _____ are in the north.
5. _____ buttons in the elevator. _____ have lights inside them.
6. _____ a famous park in New York. _____ has a lot of big trees.
7. _____ some beautiful birds in the zoo. _____ come from the tropics.
8. _____ a small piano in the hall. _____ is for the student program tonight.

C. -er = a person

Example: Mr. Brown is a **teacher**. He **teaches** English.

Add **-er** to each word. Then put the new words in the blanks. Use the plural if it is necessary.

play	work	farm	box
interpret	speak	listen	sing

1. Keiko is an _____ . She speaks both Japanese and English.
2. Mr. and Mrs. Clark are _____ . They have a large cotton farm.
3. Sarah Green is a wonderful _____ . She sings in Europe and North America.

4. There are seven Arabic _____ in the class.
5. Bill is not a good _____ . He talks all the time and doesn't listen.
6. Abdullah is a very good soccer _____ .

D. Compound Words

A compound word is two words together. They make one word. The meaning is like the meaning of the two words.

> Example: **sun + light = sunlight** (light from the sun)

Put the right words in the blanks.

summertime	seafood	daytime	yellowtail
sunlight	underline	stoplight	bedroom

1. Mary likes fish and other _____ . She doesn't eat very much meat.
2. Read each sentence. Put a circle around the subject. _____ the verb.
3. Most people work during the _____ . A few people work at night.
4. Be careful when you drive. If the _____ is red, you must stop.
5. People eat in the dining room. They sleep in the _____ .

E. Context Clues

These words are in the next unit. Don't use your dictionary. Choose the meaning of the boldface (dark) word.

1. Paul was born twenty-five years **ago**. He is 25 years old.
   a. again   c. before now
   b. after today   d. leave

2. We don't need these papers any more. Let's **burn** them.
   a. put them in the fire   c. keep them
   b. put them in the desk   d. store them

3. You can see beautiful pictures at an art **museum**. You can see things about science at a science **museum**. Most museums belong to the government.
   a. a building with beautiful and interesting things to look at
   b. a store that sells paintings and other beautiful things
   c. an aquarium or zoo
   d. a place where scientists work

4. Ann studied very hard for the test today. She is a good student. She will **probably** get a good grade.
   a. maybe
   b. cannot
   c. 50 percent sure
   d. almost 100 percent sure

5. You cannot drink most river water. If you drink it, you may get a **disease**.
   a. fish
   b. sickness
   c. sea animals
   d. thirsty

6. Cotton is an important **crop** in Egypt. Vegetables are an important **crop** in parts of Mexico. Coffee is an important **crop** in Brazil.
   a. plants that farmers grow
   b. plants near a house
   c. something a country buys from another country
   d. food that a farmer grows

7. The **soil** near the Nile River is very rich. There are also water and sun. There are many farms there, and the plants grow very well.
   a. good clean water
   b. dirt or land
   c. sunshine
   d. fruit and vegetables

8. It is **around** 25°C (25 degrees Celsius) today.
   a. hot
   b. cold
   c. in a circle
   d. about

9. Many Brazilian farmers **raise** coffee on their farms.
   a. grow
   b. find
   c. pick up
   d. enjoy

10. There are streets in a city. There are roads between small towns. There are **highways** between important cities.
    a. up above
    b. large, wide roads
    c. small streets
    d. airplanes

11. It is 2:56. It is **nearly** 3:00.
    a. beside
    b. inside
    c. almost
    d. after

12. Tom is a mechanic. He works in a large garage. He **earns** $15.00 an hour.
    a. fixes cars
    b. gets money for work
    c. gets tired
    d. pays

13. Some plants are poisonous. The poison is **natural** in the plants. No one puts it there.
    a. something made by people
    b. something not made by people
    c. something in the ocean
    d. something on farms

Unit III

PLANTS

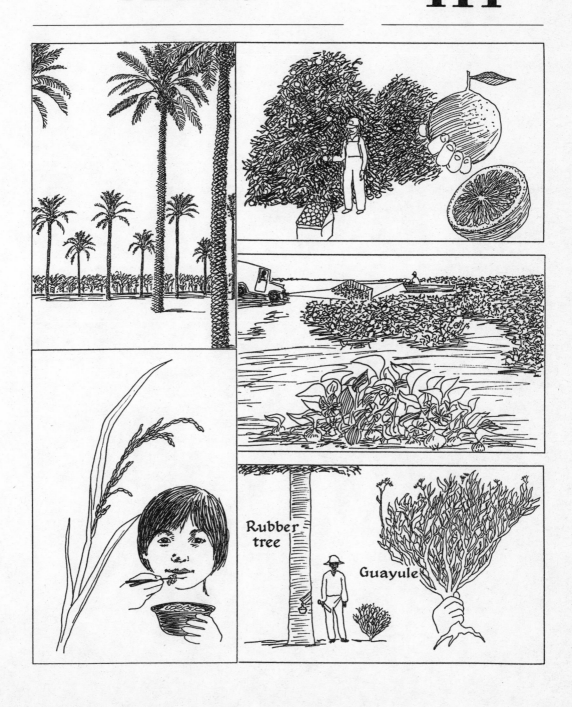

Rubber tree

Guayule

THE DATE PALM

The **date palm** is a wonderful tree. People eat dates. They feed them to their animals. They use the **leaves** and **wood** to build houses. They use the wood to build boats. They make **baskets**
5 from the leaves. They **burn** the other parts of the tree so they can cook food.

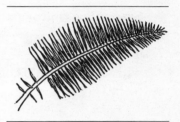

before now

The date palm came from the Middle East. Seven thousand (7,000) years **ago**, people in Syria and Egypt ate dates. They made pictures of date
10 palms on their **stone** buildings. Today date palms grow in the Middle East, parts of Asia and Africa, **southern** Europe, and other warm parts of the world.

adjective for *south*

There are more than one hundred kinds of
15 palm trees. Most of them cannot grow in the Middle East because it is too dry. The date palm grows there very well.

Hundreds of years ago people in southern Europe and Arab countries made pictures of palm
20 trees and palm flowers on some of their buildings. Today we can see these pictures in **art museums**. People think that the palm tree is beautiful. People thought the same thing a long time ago.

A. Vocabulary

burn	date palm	southern	art
leaves	grow	wood	museums
ago	buildings	baskets	stone

1. Today we can see these pictures in _____ _____ .
2. They use the _____ and _____ to build houses.
3. Today date palms grow in the Middle East, parts of Asia and Africa, _____ Europe, and other warm parts of the world.
4. The _____ is a wonderful tree.
5. They_____ the other parts of the tree so they can cook food.
6. Seven thousand years _____ , people in Syria and Egypt ate dates.
7. They make _____ from the leaves.
8. They made pictures of date palms on their _____ buildings.

B. Vocabulary (new context)

southern	wood	basket	art
museum	ago	dates	stone
palm	burn	leaves	think

1. Some trees have very large green _____ .
2. Argentina is in the _____ part of South America.
3. Marie started to study English five years _____ .
4. Stone cannot _____ . Wood can.
5. People burn _____ to make a fire.
6. A science _____ is a very interesting place.
7. There is a _____ of fruit on the table.
8. Pam has a small _____ in her shoe. It hurts.
9. One kind of _____ tree gives oil. People make soap from it.
10. People dry _____ and keep them for a long time.
11. Michelangelo was an artist. His _____ is very famous.

C. Vocabulary Review

both	stars	difficult	so
deaf	each other	idea	whole
sign	interpreter	dance	heat
weigh	stomach	believe	could

1. An _____ speaks two languages.
2. Do you _____ that there are farms in the sea?
3. There are a lot of _____ out tonight. The sky is beautiful.
4. They _____ not come to the party last night. They were too busy.
5. How tall are you and how much do you _____?
6. Palm trees like the _____ but not the cold.
7. The _____ says, "Please use other door."
8. A piano is a thing. Love is an _____.
9. The students usually talk to _____ between classes.
10. Bill cleaned his _____ apartment on Saturday.
11. The hippo has a very long _____.
12. Do you like to _____?

D. Questions

1. How do people use the palm tree?
*2. What is the name of the fruit of the palm tree?
3. Where did the date palm come from?
4. When did Syrians and Egyptians start to eat dates?
5. How many kinds of palm trees are there?
6. Why can't most of them grow in the Middle East?
7. Where can we see beautiful old pictures of palm trees?
*8. Why did Syrians and Egyptians make pictures of palm trees?
9. Why do date palms grow in the Middle East?

E. Comprehension

1. People make boats from the _____ of palm trees.
   a. leaves
   b. wood
   c. dates
   d. flowers

2. They make baskets from the _____ .
   a. leaves   c. dates
   b. wood   d. flowers

3. They _____ part of the tree to make a fire.
   a. enjoy   c. burn
   b. dance   d. grow

4. The date palm came from _____ .
   a. California   c. southern Europe
   b. Africa   d. the Middle East

5. People started to eat dates about _____ years ago.
   a. a few hundred   c. 5,000
   b. 100   d. 7,000

6. Date palms grow _____ .
   a. in the land of the polar bear c. where kiwis live
   b. in hot or warm places   d. in cool places

7. There are more than _____ kinds of palm trees.
   a. a few hundred   c. 5,000
   b. 100   d. 7,000

8. People use _____ palm tree.
   a. the whole   c. almost all of the
   b. the leaves and wood of the   d. the fruit and leaves of the

F. Main Idea

1. The date palm grows in the Middle East today.
2. The date palm is beautiful, and people use all of it.
3. People made pictures of the date palm, and these pictures are in art museums now.

THE WATER HYACINTH

2

The **water hyacinth** growns in tropical countries. It has beautiful purple-blue flowers, but everybody **hates** it. Why?

≠ loves

Millions and millions of these plants grow in
5   rivers and lakes. Sometimes the plants **become so** thick that people can walk on them. People cannot travel in boats on the water, and they cannot fish in it. The plants stop the water from moving. Then the water carries **diseases**. Farmers cannot use
10   the water on their land.

sicknesses

Now scientists think that water hyacinths can be useful. The plants are really a free **crop**. No one has to take care of them. They **just** grow and grow and grow. What can farmers use them for?

plants a farmer grows

15   Some fish like to eat them. Farmers can grow these fish in the lakes and rivers.

Workers can collect and cut the plants with **machines**. Then they can make **fertilizer** to make their crops grow **better**. They can also make feed
20   for their farm animals.

Maybe it will be possible to make **methane gas** (CH_4) for **energy**. (We burn gas from petroleum for energy. Methane gas comes from plants.) Then poor tropical countries will not have to buy so
25   much expensive petroleum.

Maybe in the future people will love the water hyacinth instead of hating it.

A. Vocabulary

feed	machines	energy	hates
water hyacinth	diseases	crop	millions
so	just	lakes	methane gas
become	better	fertilizer	petroleum

1. Workers can collect and cut the plants with _____ .
2. Then they can make _____ to make their crops grow _____ .
3. Maybe it will be possible to make _____ (CH$_4$) for _____ .
4. It has beautiful purple-blue flowers, but everybody _____ it.
5. The plants are really a free _____ .
6. Then the water carries _____ .
7. Sometimes the plants _____ _____ thick that people can walk on them.
8. The _____ grows in tropical countries.
9. They _____ grow and grow and grow.

B. Vocabulary (new context)

just	hate	tropical	disease
better	petroleum	become	lakes
travel	feed	fertilizer	energy
machines	crop	so	flowers

1. Rice is an important _____ in Asia.
2. Tom became very sick with a _____ . He died.
3. A grade of 90% is _____ than 60%.
4. I am _____ tired that I can't study.
5. Patty is _____ a baby. She cannot walk.
6. Farm _____ make the work easier.
7. Many farmers in China make their own _____ .
8. Some students _____ to study. They just want to have a good time.
9. Mary wants to _____ an engineer.
10. We use gas and oil for _____ .

C. Vocabulary Review
Match the words that mean the same.

Column A

1. also _____
2. difficult _____
3. modern _____
4. both _____
5. enjoy _____
6. toward _____
7. deaf _____
8. expensive _____
9. percent _____
10. group _____

Column B

a. two
b. can't hear
c. not cheap
d. not easy
e. %
f. leaves
g. like
h. too
i. new
j. own
k. to
l. several

D. Questions

1. Where does the water hyacinth grow?
2. Why do people hate this plant? Tell three reasons.
3. Water hyacinths are a free crop. What does this mean?
4. How can people use water hyacinths? Tell four ways.
5. What is the difference between methane gas and other gas?
*6. Cheap energy is very important for poor countries. Why?

E. Comprehension: True/False

_____ 1. Water hyacinths grow very thick on some tropical lakes and rivers.

_____ 2. Sometimes the water under the plants cannot move.

_____ 3. Water hyacinths help make water clean.

_____ 4. Maybe farmers can use water hyacinths.

_____ *5. Water hyacinths grow in parts of Asia and Africa.

_____ 6. Some kinds of fish like to eat water hyacinths.

_____ 7. Water hyacinths can make petroleum.

_____ *8. These plants can give farmers more money.

F. Main Idea

Match the details with the main ideas. Write the letter under the correct main idea. Two details do not belong under a main idea.

1. People hate water hyacinths.   **2. Water hyacinths can be useful.**

a. Some fish like to eat them.
b. The plants stop the water from moving.
c. People cannot travel on the water.
d. People can make fertilizer out of them.
e. Maybe people can make methane gas.
f. They have beautiful flowers.
g. People can feed them to animals.
h. We burn gas from petroleum for energy.
i. People cannot fish.
j. The water carries diseases.

RICE

3

People all over the world eat **rice**. Millions of people in Asia, Africa, and South America eat it every day of their lives. Some people eat almost nothing but rice.

5　　Rice is a kind of **grass**. There are more than 7,000 kinds of rice. Most kinds are water plants. Farmers grow rice in many countries, **even** in the southern part of the Soviet Union and in **eastern** Australia.

10　No one really knows where rice came from. Some scientists think it started to grow in two places. They think that one kind of rice grew in southern Asia thousands of years ago. Someone in China wrote about it almost 5,000 years ago.

15　Another kind **probably** grew in **West** Africa. Other scientists think rice came from India, and Indian travelers took it to other parts of the world.

　　　There are two main ways to grow rice. Upland rice grows in dry **soil**. Most rice grows in wet soil.

20　People in many countries do all of the work by hand. This is the same way farmers worked hundreds of years ago. Some countries now use machines on their rice farms. The farmers all use fertilizer. Some **insects** are enemies of rice.

25　Farmers poison them.

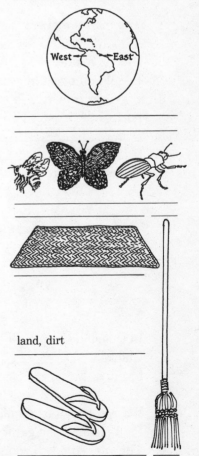

land, dirt

People use every part of the rice plant. They make animal feed and rice oil from it. They also make baskets, **brooms**, **rugs**, **sandals**, and **roofs** for their houses. They burn dry rice plants for 30 cooking.

A. Vocabulary

brooms	grass	probably	West
rice	rugs	eastern	soil
sandals	even	roofs	insects

1. They also make baskets, _____ , _____ , _____ , and _____ for their houses.
2. Rice is a kind of _____ .
3. People all over the world eat _____ .
4. Farmers grow rice in many countries, _____ in the southern part of the Soviet Union and in _____ Australia.
5. Some _____ are enemies of rice.
6. Another kind _____ grew in _____ Africa.
7. Upland rice grows in dry _____ .

B. Vocabulary (new context)

even	probably	rice	eastern
rug	sandals	grass	insects
roof	soil	West	broom

1. In the summer people like to wear _____ instead of shoes.
2. Chicken, _____ , and salad make a good dinner.
3. Frank is two years old. He wants to play basketball but he can't _____ pick up the ball.
4. We can have our picnic on the _____ under that tree.
5. Paul cleaned the garage floor with a _____ .
6. The rain comes through the _____ of the old house.
7. Korea is in the _____ part of Asia.

8. Some _____ live together in a group.
9. Lebanon is in _____ Asia.
10. There are a lot of black clouds in the sky. It will _____ rain.
11. Plants must have sun, water, and good _____ .
12. Mr. and Mrs. Cook have a beautiful new _____ for the living room floor.

C. Vocabulary Review
Match the words that mean the opposite.

Column A

1. already _____
2. large _____
3. toward _____
4. enemy _____
5. difficult _____
6. hate _____
7. cheap _____
8. collect _____
9. heat _____
10. southern _____

Column B

a. easy
b. cold
c. not yet
d. northern
e. small
f. friend
g. each other
h. away from
i. pass out
j. wood
k. expensive
l. love

D. Questions

*1. Why do some people eat almost nothing but rice?
*2. In what countries is rice an important food?
3. What kind of plant is rice?
4. How many kinds of rice are there?
5. Scientists have two ideas about where rice came from. What are they?
*6. What does "upland" mean?
*7. Why do rice farmers use fertilizer?
*8. Why do most farmers grow rice by hand?
9. How do farmers kill insects?
10. People eat rice. Tell other ways people use the rice plant.

E. Comprehension: True/False/No Information

_____ 1. Rice is a kind of grass.
_____ 2. Rice grows on dry land and in wet soil.
_____ 3. Scientists know that rice came from India.
_____ 4. Rice grows in the United States.
_____ 5. There are more than 7,000 kinds of rice.
_____ 6. Maybe Chinese travelers took rice to India.
_____ 7. More people grow rice with machines than by hand.
_____ 8. Farmers use fertilizer to kill insects.
_____ 9. Chinese farms need more fertilizer than Indian farms.
_____ 10. People use every part of the rice plant.

F. Main Idea

1. Rice is a very important crop but nobody knows where it came from.
2. People grow rice in many countries.
3. Today rice farmers use machines, fertilizer, and poisons.

ORANGES

4

Everybody loves oranges. They are **sweet** and juicy. They are in **sections** so it is easy to eat them. Some oranges do not have any **seeds**. Some have a thick **skin** and some have a **thin** skin.

5   The orange tree is beautiful. It has a lot of **shiny** green leaves. The small white flowers smell very sweet. An orange tree has flowers and fruit at the same time.

    There were orange trees twenty million years
10 ago. The oranges were very small, not like the ones today. The orange tree probably came from China. Many different kinds of **wild** oranges grow there today. Chinese started to **raise** orange trees **around** 2400 B.C. Chinese art has **lovely** old
15 pictures of oranges and orange trees.

    Farmers in other parts of Asia and the Middle East learned to raise oranges from the Chinese. Then they taught Europeans. The Spanish plant-ed orange trees in the New World (North and
20 South America). They took them to Florida first. Oranges are a very important crop in Florida today.

    "Orange" is both a fruit and a color. The color of oranges is so beautiful that in English we use the
25 name of the fruit for the color.

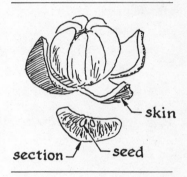

not planted by people
grow
about

A. Vocabulary

around	wild	sections	lovely
skin	oranges	raise	smell
seeds	shiny	thin	sweet

1. Chinese started to _____ orange trees _____ 2400 B.C.
2. They are _____ and juicy.
3. Some have a thick _____ and some have a _____ skin.
4. Many different kinds of _____ oranges grow there today.
5. They are in _____ so it is easy to eat them.
6. Chinese art has _____ old pictures of oranges and orange trees.
7. Some oranges do not have any _____ .
8. It has a lot of _____ green leaves.

B. Vocabulary (new context)

oranges	lovely	sweet	wild
sections	raise	shines	leaves
seeds	around	thin	skin

1. Japanese _____ fish on farms in the sea.
2. The Syrians made _____ pictures of date palms on stone buildings.
3. Plants grow from _____ .
4. A bird has feathers on its _____ . A camel has hair.
5. The polar bear and hippo are _____ animals.
6. There are three _____ of the beginning class.
7. The sun _____ every day in the desert.
8. Dates and oranges are _____ .
9. Carlos is fat. Paulo is _____ .
10. People started eating date _____ 7,000 years ago.

C. Vocabulary Review

interpreter	museums	become	better
diseases	energy	gas	grass
west	east	broom	roof
even	insects	sandals	soil

1. Sweden is _____ of Norway and _____ of Finland.
2. Students always _____ very busy at the end of the semester.
3. Many kinds of _____ eat farmers' crops.
4. The Sousas have _____ all around their house. There are also flowers and trees.
5. Desert _____ is very dry.
6. We can get some _____ from drinking dirty water.
7. Tom looked everywhere for his dictionary. He _____ looked in his car.
8. Roberto is an _____ . He works in Geneva.
9. Tourists usually go to art _____ to see beautiful pictures.
10. Your feet feel cool when you wear _____ .
11. Lois is a _____ student than Helen. Helen is not a good student.
12. The _____ is on the outside of the house. The ceiling is on the inside.

D. Questions

1. Describe an orange.
2. Do all oranges have seeds?
3. Describe an orange tree.
4. Where did the orange tree probably come from?
5. Who plants wild orange trees?
6. How did Europeans learn to raise oranges?
7. How did the United States get orange trees?
8. What else does "orange" describe?
*9. Why did people in Saudi Arabia eat dates instead of oranges?

E. Comprehension

1. Oranges are _____ .
   a. shiny and green
   b. old and wild
   c. sweet and juicy
   d. thin and white

2. Some oranges do not have _____ .
   a. seeds
   b. sections
   c. flowers
   d. a skin

3. Orange leaves are _____ .
   a. shiny
   b. thick
   c. sweet
   d. wild

4. There are many _____ orange trees in China today.
   a. shiny
   b. thin
   c. wild
   d. thick

5. Europeans learned to plant orange trees from _____ .
   a. the Middle East
   b. Florida
   c. North and South America
   d. the Spanish

*6. Oranges do not grow in _____ .
   a. India
   b. Sweden
   c. Mexico
   d. North Africa

F. Main Idea

1. Oranges are sweet and juicy with seeds and a skin.
2. Orange trees went from Asia to the Middle East to Europe to the New World.
3. Oranges probably came from China, and today people all over the world like them because they are sweet and juicy.

GUAYULE

5

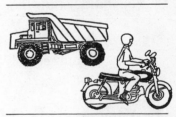

Rubber is very important in the modern world. We use it for **tires** for automobiles, buses, **trucks**, **motorcycles**, and airplanes. We use large trucks and other machines to build **highways**.
5 They have large rubber tires.

Natural rubber comes from trees. Most of the world's rubber comes from Malaysia, Indonesia, and Thailand in Southeast Asia. We also make rubber from petroleum. This kind of rubber
10 becomes hot very fast. We can use it for only some kinds of tires.

Now scientists can make rubber from **guayule**. This wild plant grows in northern Mexico and the southwestern United States. It doesn't need
15 very much rain. It can grow in desert soil. Guayule rubber is **nearly** the same as rubber from the rubber tree.

almost

Indians in Arizona **plan** to start guayule farms. They know a lot about farming in the desert.
20 The farms will use poor desert land and give people **jobs**. The Indians think they can make a lot of money from guayule rubber.

work

Poor desert countries in Africa could grow guayule too. People could **earn** money on their
25 own desert land. If they grow their own rubber, they will not have to buy it from other countries.

A. Vocabulary

natural	plan	jobs	earn
guayule	tires	nearly	airplanes
rubber	motorcyles	trucks	highways

1. _____ rubber comes from trees.
2. We use it for _____ for automobiles, buses, _____ , _____ , and airplanes.
3. People could _____ money on their own desert land.
4. Now scientists can make rubber from _____ .
5. We use large trucks and other machines to build _____ .
6. Indians in Arizona _____ to start guayule farms.
7. Guayule rubber is _____ the same as rubber from the rubber tree.
8. _____ is very important in the modern world.
9. The farms will use poor desert land and give people _____ .

B. Vocabulary (new context)

rubber	tire	naturally	nearly
southwestern	earn	plan	motorcycle
truck	airplanes	highways	jobs

1. Antonia works for the government. She doesn't _____ very much money.
2. Glen drives a _____ . He is a truck driver.
3. It is _____ time for dinner.
*4. My car needs a new _____ .
5. Children like to play with a _____ ball.
6. What do you _____ to study after you learn English?
7. Some students have part-time _____ . They earn a little money.
8. Most countries have good _____ around the capital city.
9. George had a bicycle. Now he has a _____ . Next he wants to buy a car.
10. Sea water is _____ salty. No one puts salt in it.

C. Vocabulary Review
Underline the word that does not belong.

1. oranges, water hyacinth, dates, rice
2. driver, interpreter, farmer, cheaper
3. burn, enjoy, have fun, like
4. cloud, moon, star, sun
5. wood, gas, stone, oil
6. south, east, west, northern
7. sugar, date, orange, rice
8. wild, wonderful, beautiful, lovely
9. broom, machine, roof, sandals
10. leaves, flowers, fruit, insects

D. Questions

1. What do we use rubber for?
2. Where does natural rubber come from?
3. What countries grow most of the world's rubber?
4. Some rubber is made from petroleum. Why can't we use it for all kinds of tires?
5. Where does guayule grow wild?
*6. What is the land like there?
7. Who is going to grow guayule on farms in Arizona?
8. How will the farms help the Indians?
9. What other countries could grow guayule?
10. Why is it good for desert countries in Africa to grow their own rubber?
*11. Why does the modern world use a lot of rubber?
*12. Rubber trees don't grow in Europe. Why?
*13. Do Africans understand desert farming?

E. Comprehension: True/False/No Information

_____ 1. Rubber grows in Sri Lanka and India.
_____ 2. Bicycles have rubber tires.
_____ 3. Motorcycles have rubber tires.
_____ 4. All rubber comes from trees.

_____ 5. Rubber trees have shiny leaves.

_____ 6. Guayule is a desert plant that grows in North America.

_____ 7. Guayule is nearly the same as a water hyacinth.

_____ 8. There are a lot of Indians in Arizona.

_____ 9. Guayule needs rich soil and lots of water.

_____ 10. Guayule farms could make jobs for people.

F. Main Idea

1. We can get rubber from guayule instead of rubber trees.
2. Guayule grows in northern Mexico and the southwestern United States.
3. Rubber is important in modern life.

WORD STUDY

A. Past Tense

Add **-ed** to most verbs for the past tense. If the verb ends in **e**, just add **d**.

        smell – smelled   raise – raised

        earn – earned   hate – hated

Use the **y** rules (see p. 23).

        study – studied   play – played

Use the 1-1-1 (one-one-one) rule (see p. 24).

        plan – planned   shop – shopped

Some verbs are irregular. You must memorize them.

Simple	Past	Simple	Past	Simple	Past
come	came	eat	ate	grow	grew
make	made	become	became	think	thought
teach	taught	take	took	be	was, were

Put the past tense of the verb in each sentence.

(eat)   1. We _____ lunch at 1:00 yesterday.

(plan)   2. This morning Jeff _____ his whole day.

(take)   3. Ms. Mendez _____ her daughter to the doctor yesterday.

(be)   4. Paul _____ nearly late for class this morning.

(carry)   5. Robert _____ his baggage into the airport.

(think)   6. We _____ about the problem for a long time last week.

(come)   7. Alice _____ to our party last Saturday.

(teach)   8. Mr. Cook _____ in Japan for six years. Now he teaches in New York.

(become)   9. Paula studied at the university for eight years. Last year she _____ a doctor.

(grow)   10. The Larsons _____ cotton on their land for ten years. Now they grow guayule.

(shop)   11. Ali _____ for three hours last night.

(make)   12. Donna _____ bread yesterday.

(dance)   13. The students _____ a long time at the party last Friday night.

B. Comparisons

We add -**er** to short adjectives (words with one syllable) to compare two things. We use **than**. We use **more than** with most longer words (words with three or more syllables).

Example: Sally is **more beautiful than** Ann.
Rice is **more important than** potatoes in China.

Irregular: **good – better**   **bad – worse**   **far – farther**
A car is **better than** a bicycle.
A bicycle is **worse than** a car.
An airplane can go **farther than** a car.

Write the correct form of the adjective. Then write **than**.

Example: (interesting)   New York is **more interesting than** Chicago.

(expensive) 1. A car is _____ a motorcycle.
(sweet)   2. Sugar is _____ oranges.
(good)   3. Oranges are _____ than grapefruit.
(thin)   4. Bill is _____ Paul.
(difficult) 5. French is _____ Spanish.
(small)   6. A date is _____ an orange.
(intelligent) 7. Ruth is _____ Tom.
(wonderful) 8. A trip to the moon is _____ a trip to the supermarket.
(far)   9. If you are in New York, Dallas is _____ Chicago.

C. Plural Nouns

Most of the rules for adding **s** to nouns are the same as the rules for adding **s** to verbs.

baby   – babies   bus – buses
highway – highways   lunch – lunches

If a noun ends in **f**, change the **f** to **v** and add -**es**. If a noun ends in **fe**, change the **f** to **v** and add -**s**.

leaf   – leaves   life – lives

Irregular: roof – roofs

Write the plural for each noun.

lunch	leaf	crop	enemy
roof	sandal	seed	tire
knife	day	family	match
key	dress	aquarium	library

D. -y adjectives
Add -y to some nouns or verbs to make an adjectcive.

cloud – cloudy   sun – sunny

Use the 1-1-1 rule.

sun – sunny   But: snow – snowy

If the word ends in **e**, drop the **e** and add **y**.

shine – shiny   ice – icy

Add **y** to each word. Be careful of the spelling. Then choose the right word for each sentence.

salt	snow	juice	sun
ice	cloud	wind	shine

1. Yesterday was a beautiful day. It was _____ . The sky is _____ today. The weather is bad.
2. Oranges are _____ . Bananas are not.
3. Gold is _____ .
4. In winter there are often _____ days. Sometimes the streets become _____ .
5. In spring there are _____ days. The wind blows a lot.
6. This food is too _____ . I can't eat it.

E. Context Clues

1. Sarah is in the hospital. I plan to **visit** her this afternoon.
    a. help
    b. go to see
    c. hate
    d. drive to her house

2. There is a movie **theater** only a kilometer from my house. I go to the movies there often.
   a. building for movies
   b. good movie
   c. stadium
   d. gymnasium

3. Most rice grows in water or wet soil. **However**, some rice grows on dry land.
   a. and
   b. so
   c. if
   d. but

4. The class finishes at 10:50. It is 10:45 now, and the class will finish **soon**.
   a. tomorrow
   b. later
   c. in a short time
   d. early

5. Cola drinks are **popular** all over the world.
   a. people like them
   b. natural
   c. people hate them
   d. possible

6. We eat bananas and oranges **raw**. We do not usually eat meat **raw**.
   a. in the morning
   b. for lunch
   c. lovely
   d. not cooked

7. People started to make things with machines during the **century** from 1800 to 1900.
   a. ten years
   b. fifty years
   c. hundred years
   d. thousand years

8. When you **add** two and two, you get four.
   a. +
   b. −
   c. ×
   d. ÷

9. This is a poor movie. It is very slow and **boring**.
   a. good
   b. not interesting
   c. not fast
   d. lovely

10. Sugar is a **sweetener**. We put it in candy, desserts, and ice cream.
    a. It makes something soft.
    b. It makes something fresh.
    c. It makes something sweet.
    d. It makes something better.

11. Mr. Baker has his own **company**. The company sells fruit and vegetables to supermarkets.
   a. business
   b. motorcycle
   c. car
   d. job

12. **Artificial** house plants look like plants, but they are plastic.
   a. old
   b. new
   c. not pretty
   d. not natural

13. Oscar usually listens to the car radio **while** he drives to class.
   a. after
   b. before
   c. when
   d. but

14. Alexander Graham Bell **invented** the telephone. There were no phones before that.
   a. made the first one
   b. called
   c. talked on
   d. sold

Unit IV

POPULAR FOOD

Sandwich

Pizza

Potato chips

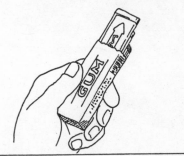

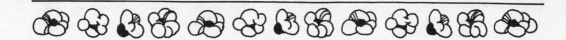

POPCORN

1

Indians in North and South America ate popcorn thousands of years ago. Scientists found some
ears of popcorn in New Mexico, a state in the United
States. They were 5,600 years old. Farmers probably
5 learned to raise popcorn first before they planted
other kinds of corn. Farmers now raise popcorn in the
United States, Australia, Argentina, South Africa,
and southern Europe.

Corn was in important food for the Indians. It
10 was also important for their **religion**. When Columbus and other Europeans **visited** the New World,
they saw this. When the Indians and Europeans had
their first **Thanksgiving**, they ate popcorn. Today
Thanksgiving is an important **holiday** in the United
15 States, but people don't usually eat popcorn for this
holiday now.

Many Europeans and Indians fought **wars** with
each other. When a war finished, the Indians brought
popcorn as a sign of **peace**.

20 In the 1920s, people started selling popcorn at
movies. Now most movie **theaters** in the United
States sell popcorn. Popcorn and movies go together very well. During the Second World War,
American **soldiers** in the **army** taught Europeans to
25 eat popcorn.

but

Is popcorn good for you? Yes, it is. **However**,
some people put a lot of salt and butter or vegetable
oil on it. It **tastes** good that way, but it is not very
good for you.

A. Vocabulary

peace	wars	religion	however
visited	theaters	army	holiday
popcorn	Thanksgiving	tastes	soldiers

1. It was also important for their _____ .
2. Now most movie _____ in the United States sell popcorn.
3. When the Indians and Europeans had their first_____ , they ate popcorn.
4. _____ , some people put a lot of salt and butter or vegetable oil on it.
5. When Columbus and other Europeans_____ the New World, they saw this.
6. Many Europeans and Indians fought _____ with each other.
7. When a war finished, the Indians brought popcorn as a sign of

   _____ .
8. It _____ good that way, but it is not very good for you.
9. Today Thanksgiving is an important _____ in the United States.
10. During the Second World War, American _____ in the _____ taught Europeans to eat popcorn.

B. Vocabulary (new context)

holiday	religion	however	peace
tastes	visit	theater	army
brought	soldier	War	Thanksgiving

1. Ali is a Muslim. This is his _____ . Maria is a Christian.
2. A date _____ sweeter than an orange.
3. We can make rubber from petroleum._____ , we cannot use it for all kinds of tires.
4. The movie starts at 7:30. I will meet you at the_____ at 7:15.
5. Our children _____ their grandparents every week.
6. Bob was in the _____ for four years. He was a

   _____ .

7. The Second World _____ started in 1939. It ended in 1945 and there was _____ .

8. People in the United States have a big dinner on_____ . This is a very important family _____ .

C. Vocabulary Review

truck	job	rubber	natural
plan	skin	sections	palm
earth	mixed	evaporates	fresh
music	only	weighs	stomach

1. Helen has a new _____ . She will work at the university.
2. Seats in some _____ of the stadium are expensive.
3. The Jensens _____ to go to Japan next summer.
4. Pat's hair is not really blond. The _____ color is brown.
5. The moon travels around the _____ once every twenty-four hours.
6. If you leave water out in the sun, it _____ .
7. Food stays in your _____ for several hours.
8. Students from different countries are _____ together in the same class.
9. _____ fruit and vegetables are good for you. Eat some every day.
10. A hippopotamus _____ more than a camel.
11. You can hear _____ on the radio twenty-four hours a day.
12. People from different parts of the world have different color _____ .

D. Questions

1. Where did popcorn come from?
2. How was corn important to Indians?
3. Name an important holiday in the United States.
4. Why did Indians give popcorn to Europeans at the end of a war?
5. When did movie theaters start selling popcorn?

6. When did people in Europe start eating popcorn?
7. Where do farmers grow popcorn?
8. Is popcorn good for you? When isn't it good for you?
*9. What do people have with their popcorn at a movie theater? Why?

E. Comprehension

1. The ears of corn in New Mexico were _____ years old.
   a. thousands of   c. 1920
   b. hundreds of   d. 5,600

2. Corn was important for the Indians' _____ .
   a. religion   c. holidays
   b. lives   d. a and b

3. Indians gave popcorn to the Europeans _____ .
   a. on the first Thanksgiving   c. at the end of a war
   b. at a movie theater   d. a and c

4. People like to eat popcorn _____ .
   a. in class   c. at school
   b. at the movies   d. at work

5. American _____ taught Europeans to eat popcorn.
   a. farmers   c. scientists
   b. truck drivers   d. soldiers

6. Is popcorn good for you?
   a. yes   c. no
   b. always   d. a and c

*7. A lot of salt and butter is _____ .
   a. good for you   c. expensive
   b. not good for you   d. cheap

HAMBURGERS

Everybody knows that the hamburger is a very **popular** American food. However, people in the United States learned to make hamburgers from Germans. The Germans got the idea from
5 Russia.

In the thirteenth **century** the Tartar people from Central Asia moved into Russia and parts of Europe. They fought the Russians and **won**. They ate something like hamburger meat, but it was
10 **raw**. This raw meat was beef, **lamb, goat** meat, or horsemeat. **Soon** the Russians started to eat raw meat too. Germans from Hamburg and other northern cities learned to eat this food from the Russians. However, they **added salt, pepper**, a
15 raw egg, and then cooked it.

Between 1830 and 1900 thousands of Germans went to live in the United States. They took the hamburger with them. People called it hamburg steak.

20 In 1904 at the World's **Fair** in St. Louis (a city on the Mississippi River), a man from Texas sold hamburger steak in a **roll**. Then people could eat it with their hands, like a sandwich. This was the first real hamburger like the hamburgers we eat today.

25 Today some people still like to eat raw beef. They call it "steak tartare."

100 years

not cooked
in a short time

added = put in, +

a kind of bread

A. Vocabulary

hamburger	pepper	popular	roll
lamb	century	Fair	added
goat	raw	soon	won

1. In the thirteenth _____ the Tartar people from Central Asia moved into Russia and parts of Europe.
2. Everybody knows that the hamburger is a very _____ American food.
3. _____ the Russians started to eat raw meat too.
4. In 1904 at the World's _____ in St. Louis, a man from Texas sold hamburg steak in a _____ .
5. They ate something like hamburger meat, but it was _____ .
6. This raw meat was beef, _____ , _____ meat or horsemeat.
7. However, they _____ salt, _____ , a raw egg, and then cooked it.
8. They fought the Russians and _____ .

B. Vocabulary (new context)

century	goats	add	hamburger
pepper	roll	popular	lamb
fairs	soon	raw	won

1. _____ is the meat from sheep. It is also the word for a young sheep.
2. There are one hundred years in a _____ .
3. Some people like to have a _____ and butter with their dinner.
4. Some desert people raise sheep and _____ .
5. Canadians often put salt and _____ on their food.
6. Most countries have _____ in the fall. Farmers show their plants and animals. Old friends see each other.
7. Can you _____ these numbers? $456 + 142 + 862 = ?$
8. The dolphin is a _____ animal at an aquarium.
9. Which team _____ the basketball game?

10. We do not cook a salad. We eat it _____ .
11. Keiko will finish her English course _____ . She will finish in two weeks.

C. Vocabulary Review
Match the words that mean the same.

Column A
1. theater _____
2. however _____
3. visit _____
4. soldier _____
5. natural _____
6. lovely _____
7. thin _____
8. rice _____
9. highway _____
10. roof _____
11. sandal _____
12. earn _____
13. war _____

Column B
a. someone in the army
b. the top of a house
c. not made by people
d. get money for work
e. peace
f. a building for movies
g. go to see
h. beautiful
i. fighting
j. a wide road
k. not fat
l. smell
m. an important food for some people
n. but
o. a kind of shoe

D. Questions

1. Who taught Americans about hamburgers?
2. Where did Germans learn about them?
*3. Where does the name "hamburger" come from?
4. Where did the Tartars come from?
5. What kind of meat did they eat?
6. How did the Germans change this Tartar meat?
7. What did Americans call hamburgers at first?
8. When did a man first put hamburger meat into a roll? Why?
*9. Do hamburgers taste good?
*10. How many centuries did it take for the Tartar raw meat to become the American hamburger?

E. Comprehension: True/False

_____ 1. Americans were the first people to eat hamburger meat.
_____ 2. Americans got hamburgers from the Russians.
_____ 3. Today Americans make hamburgers from lamb and goat meat.
_____ 4. The Tartars and Russians had a war.
_____ *5. Germans went to live in the United States during the nineteenth century.
_____ 6. Russians cooked their hamburger meat with a raw egg.
_____ 7. Hamburg is a German city.
_____ 8. People always eat a hamburger with a knife and fork.
_____ *9. The hamburger is named for a German city.
_____ *10. You can buy hamburgers in many countries.

CHEWING GUM

3

Why do people like to **chew gum**? Some people say they like the taste. Others say they can think better when they chew gum. Some people chew it when they have some **boring** work to do.

not interesting

5 Others chew gum when they are **nervous**.

Gum is a **mixture** of several things. For many years gum **companies** made gum from **chicle**. Chicle is a natural gum from a tree in Mexico and Central America. Now companies use plastic and

noun for *mix*

10 rubber made from petroleum instead of chicle.

Gum must be **soft** so you can chew it. A **softener** keeps it soft. The gum company makes the softener from vegetable oil. A **sweetener** makes the gum sweet. This sweetener is usually

≠ hard

15 sugar. Then the company adds the **flavor**.

Thomas Adams made the first gum from chicle in 1836. However, chewing gum was not new. The Greeks chewed gum from a tree over 2000 years ago. Mayan Indians in Mexico chewed

20 chicle. Indians in the northeastern United States taught Europeans to chew gum from a tree there.

People first made **bubble** gum in 1928. Children like to **blow** bubbles with bubble gum. Some university students do too.

A. Vocabulary

chew	blow	Mayan	bubble
sweetener	taste	companies	gum
softener	flavor	plastic	boring
chicle	nervous	mixture	soft

1. People first made _____ gum in 1928.
2. Gum must be _____ so you can chew it.
3. Why do people like to _____ _____ ?
4. A _____ makes the gum sweet.
5. Some people chew it when they have some _____ work to do.
6. Then the company adds the _____ .
7. Gum is a _____ of several things.
8. A _____ keeps the gum soft.
9. Others chew gum when they are _____ .
10. For many years gum _____ made gum from _____ .
11. Children like to _____ bubbles with bubble gum.

B Vocabulary (new context)

sweeten	bubbles	chew	mixture
chicle	taste	plastic	Mayan
soft	flavor	gum	boring
company	blows	nervous	soften

1. Hot chocolate is a _____ of chocolate, sugar, and milk.
2. Chocolate is one _____ of ice cream.
3. Dolores works for a large _____ in Mexico City.
4. Children like to blow soap _____ .
5. When you eat food, you _____ it. When you drink something, you don't chew it.
6. We put sugar in coffee to _____ it.
7. It is _____ to memorize vocabulary.
8. A cat has _____ hair on its body.
9. _____ comes from different kinds of trees.

10. Students are usually _____ before a big test.
11. Dried fruit is hard. Put it in water to _____ it.
12. The wind _____ a lot in the spring.

C. Vocabulary Review
Match the words that mean the opposite.

Column A

1. war _____
2. thin _____
3. holiday _____
4. raw _____
5. during _____
6. store _____
7. west _____
8. all over _____
9. spend _____
10. soon _____
11. somebody _____

Column B

a. east
b. earn
c. century
d. peace
e. fat
f. work day
g. throw away
h. after
i. nowhere
j. win
k. cooked
l. later
m. popular
n. nobody

D. Questions

1. Why do people like to chew gum? Give four reasons.
*2. Does gum help you think better?
3. What is chicle?
4. Do companies make gum from chicle now?
5. What do they use instead of chicle?
6. What does a softener do to the gum?
7. What does a sweetener do?
8. What are the four things in the gum mixture?
9. Name three groups of people who chewed gum.
10. Who likes to blow bubbles with bubble gum?
*11. Is gum good for your teeth?

E. Comprehension

1. Some people chew gum when they are _____ .
   a. fighting
   c. lovely
   b. nervous
   d. eating

2. Some people chew gum because they like the _____ .
   a. boring
   c. mixture
   b. flavor
   d. skin

3. Today companies make gum from _____ .
   a. plastic
   c. chicle
   b. rubber from petroleum
   d. a and b

4. A softener _____ something.
   a. softens
   c. sweetens
   b. burns
   d. shortens

5. Sugar is a _____ .
   a. sweetener
   c. softener
   b. mixture
   d. flavor

6. The gum company makes the softener from _____ .
   a. petroleum
   c. plastic
   b. chicle
   d. vegetable oil

7. Different _____ make gum taste different.
   a. softeners
   c. vegetable oils
   b. flavors
   d. seeds

8. Chewing gum is _____ idea.
   a. a new
   c. a wet
   b. an old
   d. a dry

9. Children _____ bubbles with bubble gum.
   a. flavor
   c. blow
   b. mix
   d. sweeten

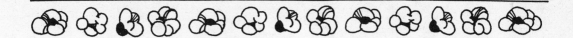

COLA DRINKS AND ICE CREAM CONES

4

The Coca-Cola company made the first cola drinks more than a hundred years ago. Companies now sell millions of **bottles** and **cans** of Coca-Cola, Pepsi-Cola, and other colas every day. The
5   cola flavor in the drinks comes from the cola or kola **nut**. These nuts grow on trees in the tropics. Kola nuts have **caffeine** in them. Coffee, tea, and chocolate have caffeine, too. Caffeine makes some people feel nervous. Now there are cola drinks
10 without caffeine.

Bottle   Can

Cola and other soft drinks have **carbon dioxide** (CO_2) in the water. This gas makes bubbles. There is also a lot of sugar in these drinks. Some soft drinks have an **artificial** sweetener
15 instead of sugar. It is possible that these artificial sweeteners are **dangerous** to the body.

not natural

The ice cream cone came from the St. Louis World's Fair in 1904, just like the hamburger. You can't eat **either** hamburger meat or ice cream in
20 your hands. Someone put hamburger meat in a roll so people could eat it in their hands. For several years, people sold ice cream between two thin cookies so people could eat it in their hands. It was like a sandwich. However, the ice cream always
25 **dripped** out. Someone made the cookie into a cone. The ice cream could not drip out and people could eat it easily with their hands.

A. Vocabulary

artificial	bottles	either	dripped
cola	caffeine	hotel	cans
dangerous	pieces	nut	carbon dioxide

1. Companies now sell millions of _____ and _____ of colas every day.
2. Some soft drinks have an _____ sweetener instead of sugar.
3. You can't eat _____ hamburger meat or ice cream in your hands.
4. The cola flavor in the drinks comes from the cola or kola _____ .
5. However, the ice cream always _____ out.
6. Kola nuts have _____ in them.
7. It is possible that these artificial sweeteners are _____ to the body.
8. Cola and other soft drinks have _____ (CO_2) in the water.

B. Vocabulary (new context)

dangerous	bottles	either	caffeine
gas	artificial	drips	nuts
carbon dioxide	bubbles	cookies	cans

1. We put _____ in candy, in desserts, and on ice cream.
2. Some people cannot sleep after they drink coffee. The _____ keeps them awake.
3. It is _____ to drive a car on icy roads.
4. CO_2 means _____ .
5. Rubber made from petroleum is _____ rubber. It is not natural rubber from trees.
6. You can buy vegetables and soup in _____ .
7. You can buy orange juice in cans and _____ .
8. The water in my shower _____ all the time. It makes me nervous.
9. You can have _____ tea or coffee after dinner. You cannot have a soft drink.

C. Vocabulary Review
Underline the word that does not belong.

1. peace, soldier, army, war
2. guayule, tree, plastic, petroleum
3. motorcycle, truck, automobile, airplane
4. add, be, come, eat
5. lamb, goat, insect, dolphin
6. century, fair, month, hour
7. seafood, underline, sunlight, mixture
8. around, eastern, southern, western
9. grass, hamburger, rice, palm

D. Questions

1. What company made the first cola drinks?
2. Where does the cola flavor come from?
3. Where do kola nuts grow?
4. What do kola nuts have in them?
5. What does CO_2 mean?
*6. Are cola drinks good for you? Why?
7. How is an ice cream cone like a hamburger?
8. Why was an ice cream cone better than an ice cream sandwich?

E. Comprehension: True/False/No Information

_____ 1. Cans of cola are cheaper than bottles.
_____ 2. Some cola drinks have caffeine in them.
_____ 3. Cola drinks have petroleum in them.
_____ 4. All cola drinks make people nervous.
_____ 5. Carbon dioxide is a gas.
_____ 6. Caffeine gives a cola drink flavor.
_____ 7. Ice cream has a softener in it.
_____ 8. An ice cream sandwich usually drips.
_____ 9. Ice cream is not good for you.

SANDWICHES, PIZZA, AND POTATO CHIPS

5

Sandwiches are **common** in many countries. Where did this strange name come from?

The Earl of Sandwich (1718–1792) was an Englishman. He liked to play **cards**. One night he
5 played for hours and got very hungry. However, he didn't want to stop his card **game**. He asked for some **roast** meat between two pieces of bread. (People **bake** roast meat in the **oven** of a stove.) He ate the food **while** he played cards. People
10 gave his name to this new kind of food.

when, at the same time

Pizza is another **international** food. A baker probably **invented** the pizza in Naples, Italy. It was at about the same time as the first sandwich. "Pizza" means "pie" in Italian. People used the
15 name "pizza pie" for a long time. Now it is just "pizza."

made the first one

Potato chips came from Saratoga Springs in New York State. In 1853 a man at a hotel in that town wanted some French **fried** potatoes. How-
20 ever, he wanted very thin ones. The cook cut some very thin pieces of potatoes and fried them in oil. Then he put salt on them. They soon became very popular. People called them Saratoga chips for a long time.

POPULAR FOOD

A. Vocabulary

oven	invented	common	fried
international	cards	while	bake
sandwich	game	roast	pieces

1. Sandwiches are _____ in many countries.
2. He asked for some _____ meat between two pieces of bread.
3. Pizza is another _____ food.
4. He ate the food _____ he played cards.
5. He liked to play _____ .
6. A baker probably _____ the pizza in Naples, Italy.
7. However, he didn't want to stop his card _____ .
8. In 1853 a man at a hotel in that town wanted some French_____ potatoes.
9. People _____ roast meat in the _____ of a stove.

B. Vocabulary (new context)

invent	common	cards	oven
baked	game	while	hungry
roast	international	fry	pieces

1. Mary usually listens to music _____ she studies.
2. Helen _____ a chocolate cake this morning.
3. Many people enjoy playing _____ .
4. Who won the soccer _____ ?
5. Sometimes we_____ meat in oil on top of the stove. We bake or _____ food in the _____ .
6. There is a dance tomorrow night for the_____ students. They are from different countries.
7. Maybe you can _____ a wonderful new machine.
8. Ice cream cones are _____ all over the world.

C. Vocabulary Review

chew	boring	job	gum
plan	blow	religion	Thanksgiving
museum	so	disease	energy
even	sections	skin	around

1. This television program is _____ . Let's turn it off. It's not interesting.
2. What is your _____ ? Are you a Christian?
3. Most American students spend _____ with their families. It is an important holiday.
4. You don't have to _____ ice cream.
5. Some people love sandwiches. They _____ have them for breakfast.
6. A baby's _____ is very soft.
7. There are _____ 200 students in the English program.
8. Do you _____ to go to the volleyball game tonight?
9. What kind of _____ do you want after you get your master's degree?
10. The book has four _____ . Each one is about a different subject.
11. There are some beautiful new photographs in the art _____ .
12. If you _____ on your coffee, it will get cooler.

D. Questions

*1. What does "(1718–1792)" mean?
2. Why did the Earl of Sandwich want roast meat and bread?
3. Where do people roast meat?
4. What city did pizza probably come from?
5. What does "pizza" mean?
6. What is Saratoga Springs?
7. How did the cook make potato chips?
*8. Why did people call them Saratoga chips?
*9. Why do people like food they can eat with their hands?
*10. In what century did a baker make the first pizza?

E. Comprehension: True/False

_____ 1. Sandwiches are an international food.
_____ *2. A hamburger is a kind of meat sandwich.
_____ 3. The Earl of Sandwich was from Italy.
_____ 4. People fry roast meat in the oven.
_____ 5. Pizza is Italian.
_____ 6. A cook invented the first potato chips in the eighteenth century.
_____ 7. People invented the first sandwich and the first pizza in the eighteenth century.
_____ 8. The first potato chip came from the United States.
_____ 9. A man at the hotel didn't want thick French fried potatoes.
_____ *10. Potato chips are good for you.

F. Main Idea and Supporting Details

Put the number of the supporting detail after the topics. Some supporting details are about more than one topic.

a. Popcorn _____   e. The Ice Cream Cone _____
b. The Hamburger _____   f. The Sandwich _____
c. Chewing Gum _____   g. Pizza _____
d. The Cola Drink _____ h. The Potato Chip _____

1. It has a softener and a sweetener.
2. The flavor comes from a nut.
3. Indians ate it.
4. It is named after a person.
5. Someone at the St. Louis World's Fair invented it.
6. Someone in Europe invented it.
7. The Russians taught the Germans how to make it.
8. People blow bubbles with one kind.
9. It started in Europe.
10. It has meat in it.
11. Something from a tree is in it.
12. It is a kind of vegetable.
13. It was important in the Indians' religion.
14. Part of it is bread.
15. It usually has sugar in it.

WORD STUDY

A. Questions: Past Tense

be: Put **was** or **were** before the complete subject.

	subject	
Example:	**Tom**	**was** home last night.
	Was Tom	home last night?

other verbs: Put **did** at the beginning of the sentence. Use the simple verb.

	subject	verb	
Example:	**The farmers**	**planted**	corn last spring.
	Did the farmers	**plant**	corn last spring?

Change these sentences to past tense questions.

1. Bell invented the telephone.
2. Indians ate popcorn thousands of years ago.
3. Their roast was in the oven for two hours.
4. Europeans and Indians fought wars with each other.
5. Indian farmers raised popcorn.
6. The cook fried some thin pieces of potato.
7. A man sold hamburgers at the St. Louis World's Fair.
8. People first made bubble gum in 1928.
9. The soft drinks were in bottles and cans.
10. Our neighbor went to San Francisco.

B. Irregular Verbs
Memorize these irregular verbs. Put the right verb form in each blank.

Simple	Past	Simple	Past
do	did	go	went
get	got	give	gave
see	saw	sell	sold

(do) 1. Carlos _____ his homework early yesterday.

(get) 2. Did you _____ a good grade on your test?

(see)   3. Helen _____ her friends at the Student Union this morning at breakfast time.

(go)   4. They _____ to the football game last Saturday.

(give)   5. We _____ our mother a birthday present every year.

(sell)   6. Did the Browns _____ their house?

(be)   7. Paul and Robert _____ at home last night.

(grow)   8. Rubber _____ in Malaysia.

(think)   9. I _____ of the answer after the teacher asked someone else.

(take)   10. Will you _____ the TOEFL next month?

(eat)   11. We _____ pizza for lunch every day.

(come)   12. All the students _____ to the class party last night.

C. -ly Adverbs

An adverb describes a verb. Many adverbs end in **-ly**. We can add **-ly** to many adjectives.

Example: slow – slowly

Spelling: If the word ends in **-y**, change the **y** to **i**.

        easy – easily   day – daily

If the word ends in **-ble**, drop the **le**.

        possible – possibly

Add **-ly** to each word. Then use the correct adverb in the blanks. Underline the verb.

easy	different	cheap	busy
happy	day	possible	warm

1. You must dress _____ in winter or you will catch a cold.

2. You can _____ do the homework in a half hour. There are only three short exercises.

3. People from Spain and Mexico speak Spanish, but they speak a little _____ .

4. Could I _____ borrow your car? I need one this afternoon.

5. The English classes meet _____ .

6. You can live _____ if you live in a dormitory, cook your own food, and ride a bicycle.

D. Word Forms: Noun and Verb = Same

Many words have the same form for both the noun and the verb. Read these words. Then choose the right word for each sentence. Use the correct verb form, and singular or plural nouns.

Verb	Noun
feed	feed
use	use
poison	poison
plant	plant
taste	taste
cook	cook
work	work
drink	drink

1. Ruth has lovely _____ in front of her house. She _____ them last spring.
2. Robert is a good _____ . He likes to bake cakes and he also _____ international dishes.
3. What are you eating? Can I have a _____ ? I never _____ that kind of food before.
4. Do you _____ coffee? Would you like a cold _____ ?
5. I have a lot of _____ to do. I _____ all day yesterday, but the _____ isn't finished.
6. Farmers buy one kind of _____ for chickens. They _____ their horses something different.

E. Context Clues

1. Marie is **un**happy this week. Her parents didn't telephone her, and she failed a test.
   a. not
   b. in
   c. very
   d. a little

2. Java is the name of one **island** in Indonesia.
   a. water with land all round it
   b. land with water all around it
   c. country
   d. mountains

3. Fishing boats sometimes come back to the land if there is a **storm**.
   a. sunshine
   b. some fish
   c. bad weather
   d. good weather

4. When the sun goes down, it gets **dark**.
   a. thick
   b. not easy
   c. soft
   d. not light

5. At my apartment house, children can use the pool in the morning and **adults** can use it in the afternoon.
   a. children
   b. teenagers
   c. men and women
   d. babies

6. Rio de Janeiro is on the east **coast** of Brazil.
   a. land with water around it
   b. mountain
   c. land near the sea
   d. lake

7. The sun **sets** at six p.m. every day in the tropics.
   a. comes up
   b. goes down
   c. softens
   d. sweetens

8. I feel very cold. What is the **temperature**?
   a. How cold or hot is it?
   b. How far away is it?
   c. What time is it?
   d. Where is it?

9. Bill and Paul planned to go to Europe together. Then Bill got sick so Paul went **alone**.
   a. He didn't go.
   b. He wanted to go.
   c. No one went with him.
   d. He went with Bill.

10. Betty's baby was born with a **terrible** disease. He lived only a few hours.
    a. good
    b. bad
    c. very good
    d. very bad

11. Try to speak English **quickly**. Don't stop and think about every word.
    a. slowly
    b. poorly
    c. fast
    d. well

Unit V

ANIMALS II

THE SAND WASP

1

The **sand wasp** lives in the state of Kansas in the United States. Today a sand wasp is very busy. She is building a place for her eggs. **<u>Unlike</u>** most animals, she is using **<u>tools</u>** for this job.

un = not

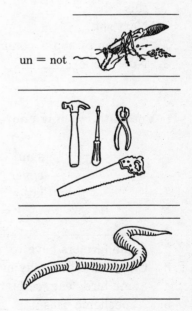

5   Now she is **<u>digging</u>** a **<u>hole</u>**. She is digging with her legs. Next she **lays** her eggs. Then she flies away.

    The sand wasp is coming back to her **nest**. She is bringing a **<u>worm</u>** with her. Now she is
10 putting the worm in the hole with the eggs.

    Now she is **covering** the hole with a small stone. She is putting **dirt** on top of the stone. She finds another stone. Now she is using this stone as a tool to push down the dirt. She brings more
15 stones and pushes down the dirt with each one. She leaves the stones there. The eggs are safe. The worm will be food for the baby wasps.

A. Vocabulary

unlike	nest	dirt	hole
wasp	lays	worm	digging
eggs	sand	covering	tools

1. Now she is _____ a _____ .
2. She is putting _____ on top of the stone.
3. The _____ _____ lives in the state of Kansas in the United States.
4. She is bringing a _____ with her.
5. _____ most animals, she is using _____ for this job.
6. Next she _____ her eggs.
7. The sand wasp is coming back to her _____ .
8. Now she is _____ the hole with a small stone.

B. Vocabulary (new context)

sand	unlike	dig	worms
cover	stone	dirty	wasp
lay	hole	tools	nest

1. A _____ is an insect.
2. Some farmers have to _____ a well to get water.
3. Children like to play in the _____ at the beach.
4. Some birds eat seeds. Others eat _____ and insects.
5. A mechanic uses _____ to fix cars.
6. Chickens _____ eggs.
7. Alan has to clean his apartment because it is very _____ .
8. There is a _____ in my shoe. I have to buy a new pair.
9. Birds and some insects build a _____ . They lay their eggs in it.
10. _____ oranges, dates can grow in the desert.
11. _____ the pans when you cook. You will save energy.

ANIMALS II

C. Vocabulary Review

game	while	common	cards
dangerous	caffeine	artificial	dripping
either	pepper	nearly	visit
theater	Thanksgiving	soon	raw

1. Restaurants in the United States have salt and _____ on each table.
2. Please sit down _____ you wait.
3. Ann is planning to visit _____ London or Paris next summer.
4. _____ fish is a common dish in Japan. Europeans cook their fish.
5. Does the _____ in coffee make you nervous?
6. My roommate has some free time and he is playing _____ with his friends. What card _____ are they playing?
7. A swimming pool is a _____ place for small children.
8. It is _____ time to go. Hurry up!
9. It rained hard and water is _____ off the roof.
10. Will your parents visit you _____ or will they be here next summer?

D. Questions

1. What is Kansas?
2. Why is the sand wasp busy today?
3. How is she different from most animals?
4. How is she digging a hole?
5. What does she do next?
6. What does she bring to her nest?
7. Why is she putting a worm in the nest?
8. How is she pushing down the dirt?
*9. Why are the eggs safe?

E. Comprehension: Sequence

The sentences below tell you how a sand wasp makes a nest and lays eggs. Number the sentences in the right order. What does she do first? What does she do second and third? The first one is done for you.

_____ She covers the hole with a small stone.

___1___ She digs a hole with her legs.

_____ She puts the worm in the hole.

_____ She lays her eggs.

_____ She puts dirt on top of the stone.

_____ She pushes the dirt down with a stone.

_____ She brings more stones to the nest.

_____ She flies away to get a worm.

_____ The baby wasps will eat the worm.

F. Main Idea

1. The sand wasp uses tools to build a nest for her eggs.
2. The sand wasp puts a worm in the nest for her babies.
3. The sand wasp works very hard.

THE ARCTIC TERN

2

It is summer in the northern part of the world. In the far north it is daylight all the time. The sun never **sets**. The arctic **terns** are laying eggs on **islands** off the **coast** of Canada. They are not
5 building nests—arctic terns don't make nests.

goes down

island = land with water all around it / coast = land by the sea

The eggs are **lying** on the sand or **rock**. The **adult** birds are flying around over them. They make an umbrella of birds. They are keeping enemies away from the eggs **below**. They do this
10 for three weeks.

stone

adult ≠ child

under

Now it is fourteen weeks later. All the birds are adults. They are flying 18,000 kilometers south. They are flying through **storms** and good weather until they **reach** Antarctica. While they
15 are flying south over the Pacific or Atlantic Ocean, they meet other terns from Northern Europe and Asia.

bad weather

Now it is winter in Canada. However, inside the Antarctic Circle in the southern part of the
20 earth, it is summer. Even in summer, it is never warm inside the Antarctic Circle, and the sun never sets. The terns are living on islands near Antarctica, eating fish and small sea animals.

Arctic terns don't like hot weather. They like
25 daylight better than the **dark**. They spend almost ten months a year flying far away from any land.

Sometimes they fly thousands of kilometers out of
the way so they can fly over cold water. They often
fly 40,000 kilometers in a year. They travel more
30   than any other animal in the world. They have more
hours of daylight than any other animal. They are
really wonderful birds.

A. Vocabulary

kilometers	sets	storms	lying
dark	terns	coast	below
reach	islands	rock	adult

1. They are flying through _____ and good weather until they _____ Antarctica.
2. The sun never _____ .
3. The eggs are _____ on the sand or _____ .
4. They like daylight better than the _____ .
5. The arctic _____ are laying eggs on _____ off the _____ of Canada.
6. The _____ birds are flying around over them.
7. They are keeping enemies away from the eggs _____ .

B. Vocabulary (new context)

reach	island	dark	daylight
adults	below	lying	coast
set	storm	Antarctica	rocky

1. University students are not children. They are _____ .
2. The people in the apartment _____ ours are very noisy.
3. Los Angeles is on the _____ of California.
4. The plane leaves at 3:00. It will _____ New York at 5:15.
5. There was a bad _____ last night. The wind blew down several trees.
6. Dan is swimming, and Tom is _____ beside the pool.

7. What time does the sun _____ tonight? It will rise at 6:30 a.m. tomorrow.

8. Some of the east coast of Canada is very _____ . There is no sand.

9. After the sun sets, it gets _____ outside and the street lights come on.

10. England is on an _____ .

C. Vocabulary Review
Match the words that mean the same.

Column A	Column B
1. unlike _____	a. usual
2. artificial _____	b. not interesting
3. while _____	c. different
4. hard _____	d. meat from sheep
5. boring _____	e. sand
6. dig _____	f. put something over
7. common _____	g. cook in the oven
8. dangerous _____	h. bottle
9. cover _____	i. when
10. bake _____	j. or
11. lamb _____	k. difficult
12. either _____	l. make a hole
	m. not natural
	n. not safe

D. Questions

*1. What are the summer months in Antarctica?

*2. What are the summer months in the Arctic?

3. Where are the terns laying their eggs?

4. Why are the terns flying above the eggs?

5. How long does it take for a baby tern to grow up?

*6. It is spring in Canada. Where are the terns flying?

7. Where do terns live while it is winter in Canada?

8. What do terns eat?
9. Do terns like hot weather? Do they like the dark?
*10. Why do arctic terns fly from the Arctic to Antarctica?
11. What do terns do so they can fly over cold water?
12. Why are arctic terns wonderful birds?

E. Comprehension

1. It is daylight all the time in the Arctic during the _____ .
   a. spring
   b. summer
   c. fall
   d. winter

*2. It is summer in Argentina and South Africa in _____ .
   a. March, April, and May
   b. June, July, and August
   c. September, October, and November
   d. December, January, and February

*3. Arctic terns spend all but _____ months a year flying.
   a. two
   b. three
   c. six
   d. ten

4. The adult lays her eggs _____ .
   a. in a nest
   b. in sand
   c. on rock
   d. b and c

5. The adults are flying over the eggs so they can keep _____ away.
   a. the rain
   b. snow
   c. enemies
   d. a and b

6. The babies grow up in _____ weeks.
   a. three
   b. six
   c. fourteen
   d. fifteen

*7. Some terns go to _____ to lay their eggs.
   a. northern Asia and Europe
   b. the southern part of the earth
   c. Antarctica
   d. Argentina

8. The terns fly around _____ kilometers from the Arctic to Antarctica.
   a. 14,000   c. 20,000
   b. 18,000   d. 40,000

9. Terns like to fly over _____ water.
   a. cold   c. warm
   b. cool   d. hot

F. Main Idea

1. The arctic tern sometimes flies 40,000 kilometers a year.
2. The arctic tern spends June, July, and August in Canada.
3. The arctic tern is the greatest animal traveler in the world.

THE SLOTH

3

It is nighttime and a mother **sloth** is moving slowly along in a tree. She is **holding on** to the tree with her long **strong** <u>claws</u>. (Animals have claws. People have <u>toenails</u>.). She is **hanging upside**
5 **down** as she moves very sl-o-o-o-w-ly through the tree. She travels about half a kilometer an hour.

Her baby is holding on to the mother's back. The baby is hanging upside down too. The baby also rides on the mother's stomach sometimes.

10 The sloth is eating some of the leaves of the tree. She eats while she is hanging upside down. She even sleeps upside down. A sloth's claws are very strong. A sloth sometimes even hangs from a tree after it dies.

15 It is difficult to see the sloths because they look like part of the tree. There are very small green plants growing in their <u>fur</u>. Insects also live in their fur.

The mother slowly climbs down to the
20 **ground**. Now she is moving even more slowly. Sloths are unhappy on the ground because it is very difficult for them to walk. A baby cannot walk **at all**.

Sloths live in Central and South America.
25 They are famous for being **lazy**. However, they are slow partly because they have a very <u>low</u> body **temperature**. It is natural for them to be slow.

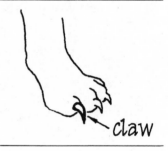

claw

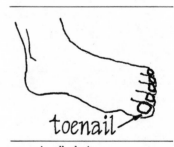

toenail

an animal's hair

low ≠ high

ANIMALS II

A. Vocabulary

nighttime	hanging	lazy	at all
temperature	dies	upside down	claws
ground	holding on	sloth	toenails
low	fur	slowly	strong

1. She is _____ _____ as she moves very
   sl-o-o-o-w-ly through the tree.
2. She is _____ to the tree with her long _____ .
3. They are famous for being _____ .
4. People have _____ .
5. However, they are slow partly because they have a very _____
   body _____ .
6. There are very small green plants growing in their _____ .
7. It is nighttime and a mother _____ is moving slowly along in a
   tree.
8. A baby cannot walk _____ .
9. The mother slowly climbs down to the _____ .

B. Vocabulary (new context)

temperature	toenails	stomach	fur
lazy	hold on	at all	low
ground	hangs	strong	upside down

1. Jean always _____ her jacket in the closet when she gets
   home.
2. Some worms live under the _____ .
3. How _____ are you? Can you pick up an elephant?
4. If you can't find a seat in the bus, you have to stand up. You also have to
   _____ to something.
5. A deaf person cannot hear anything _____ .
6. The _____ is high today. It is 40°C.
7. People have _____ on their toes and fingernails on their
   fingers.
8. Please turn your paper around. I can't read it _____ .
9. Barbara bought a beautiful expensive _____ coat.
10. Carol is _____ . She doesn't like to work.
11. Some students get high grades. Others get _____ grades.

C. Vocabulary Review

saving	rises	knives	wind
bad for	noise	awake	stars
seat	changing	rolls	pepper
goats	canned	dripping	nuts

1. Fresh fruit is better than _____ fruit.
2. Martha is _____ money for her summer vacation.
3. The sun _____ in the east and sets in the west.
4. What is that _____ ? I think I hear water _____ .
5. I couldn't go to sleep last night. I was _____ until 2:00.
6. Robert doesn't like to sit by the door so he is _____ his _____ .
7. The sky is beautiful tonight. We can see hundreds of _____ .
8. Too much sugar and salt are _____ for the body.
9. Americans usually have bread or _____ with dinner.
10. Ms. Smith gave her visitors some soft drinks, potato chips, and _____ .
11. Bobby put the plates, _____ , and forks on the table. Then he put on the salt and _____ .

D. Questions

*1. When does a sloth sleep?
2. Is the sloth standing up in the tree?
3. Why doesn't a sloth fall from a tree?
*4. What are claws?
5. How fast does she travel?
6. What is the baby doing?
7. What is the sloth eating?
8. How does she sleep?
9. Why is it hard to see the sloths?
10. What lives in their fur?
11. Why are sloths unhappy on the ground?
12. Can a baby sloth walk on the ground?
13. Where do sloths live?
*14. Are sloths lazy?
*15. Is a sloth beautiful?

E. Comprehension: True/False

_____ 1. The mother sloth is holding on to the tree with her tail.
_____ *2. A sloth hangs upside down during most of its life.
_____ 3. Sometimes a baby sloth rides on its mother's back.
_____ 4. The sloth is eating some insects.
_____ *5. A sloth holds on to a tree while she is sleeping.
_____ 6. The sloth is standing on the ground while she eats.
_____ 7. The sloth has very strong claws.
_____ *8. An enemy cannot find a sloth very easily.
_____ 9. A sloth moves more slowly on the ground than in a tree.
_____ 10. A baby sloth learns to walk when it is a week old.
_____ 11. Sloths have a high body temperature.

F. Main Idea

1. A sloth takes good care of its babies.
2. A sloth moves very slowly and spends most of its life upside down.
3. A sloth looks like part of a tree because plants and insects grow in its fur.

LOCUSTS

4

We are sitting in a village in West Africa and there are millions of **locusts** in the air, in the trees, and on the crops. They are eating every plant in front of them. They are eating both the wild plants
5 and all the crops on the farms. They are moving along slowly, **jumping** or flying from one plant to the next. Sometimes the wind carries them along **quickly**.   fast

Every few years locusts come flying out of the
10 desert. They travel on the wind from 15 to 150 kilometers a day. A locust is small. It weighs only about 60 grams. However, locusts are a **terrible**   very bad
problem because one is never **alone**. There can be 100 million of them in two square kilometers.
15 Each one eats twice its weight in food every day. Thousands of people can die after locusts **pass**   move, go
through an **area**. The locusts eat all the plants, and there is no food for the people.

Governments use airplanes to poison locusts.
20 Locusts often **appear** in Africa. The countries there do not have **enough** money to buy planes and poison. Sometimes there are wars, and the planes cannot fly to **nearby** countries to kill the   near
locusts.

ANIMALS II

25   Why do millions of locusts **suddenly** appear
out of the desert? Why do they appear every few
years? Why not every year? Why aren't there
locusts flying around farms all the time? Nobody
knows the answers to these questions. We cannot
30 **solve** the problem of locusts until we find the
answers to these questions.

A. Vocabulary

locusts	enough	terrible	jumping
quickly	solve	alone	nearby
village	problem	slowly	millions
area	appear	suddenly	pass

1. They are moving along slowly, _____ or flying from one plant
    to the next.
2. However, locusts often _____ in Africa.
3. However, locusts are a _____ _____ be-
    cause one is never _____ .
4. We cannot _____ the problem of locusts until we find the
    answers to these questions.
5. We are sitting in a village in West Africa and there are millions of
    _____ in the air, in the trees, and on the crops.
6. Thousands of people can die after locusts _____ through an

    _____ .
7. The countries there do not have _____ money to buy planes
    and poison.
8. Why do millions of locusts _____ appear out of the desert?
9. Sometimes the wind carries them along _____ .
10. Sometimes there are wars, and the planes cannot fly to _____
    countries.

B. Vocabulary (new context)

nearby	alone	appeared	suddenly
terrible	quickly	jumped	problem
passed	solve	areas	enough

1. Can you _____ this math problem? 763 × 44 = ?
2. Peter doesn't live with his family or have any roommates. He lives _____ .
3. Wars are _____ . They kill thousands of people.
4. I waited thirty minutes for Isamu and then he _____ _____ . He was sorry that he was late.
5. Ms. Johnson's children all got good grades and _____ to the next grade.
6. Water hyacinths grow in tropical _____ .
7. Do you have _____ money to buy a car?
8. Ted _____ out of the window of the burning building.
9. You have to think _____ when you are taking a test.
10. Ann lives on Peach Street and Jean lives _____ .
11. Water hyacinths are a _____ in some countries.

C. Vocabulary Review
Match the words that mean the opposite.

Column A
1. dark _____
2. soft _____
3. below _____
4. near _____
5. child _____
6. interesting _____
7. common _____
8. natural _____
9. cover _____
10. cool _____

Column B
a. ground
b. boring
c. hard
d. artificial
e. above
f. warm
g. unusual
h. adult
i. uncover
j. fur
k. light
l. far

D. Questions

1. Where are we sitting in West Africa?
2. What are the locusts doing?
3. Name three ways they travel.
4. Where do locusts come from?
5. What do they eat?
*6. How many grams of food does a locust eat every day?
7. How do locusts make people die?
8. How do governments fight locusts?
9. Why do locusts suddenly appear out of the desert?

E. Comprehension

1. The weight of a locust is about _____ grams.
   a. 30   c. 50
   b. 40   d. 60

2. Locusts are a problem because _____ .
   a. there are so many of them   c. they are so large
   b. they are so small   d. they appear from the desert

3. Locusts sometimes travel _____ .
   a. by walking   c. on the wind
   b. on water   d. by climbing

4. The wind carries them along _____ .
   a. on plants   c. jumping
   b. quickly   d. slowly

5. People die because the locusts _____ .
   a. eat all their crops   c. kill them with a kind of poison
   b. breathe all the air   d. eat all their animals

6. People kill locusts with _____ .
   a. wars   c. crops
   b. storms   d. poison

7. Maybe we can solve the problem of locusts _____ .
   a. with bigger airplanes
   b. if deserts have more rain
   c. when we know more about them
   d. if we feed them poison

F. Main Idea

1. Millions of locusts suddenly appear and eat every plant they see.
2. Locusts appear out of the desert.
3. Locusts are jumping, flying, and eating all the crops.

THE WATER SPIDER

5

A **spider** is like an insect, but it has eight legs and two parts to its body. It **spins** a **web** with **silk** from its body. Different spiders make webs with different **shapes**. Of course spiders must have air
5 to breathe.

A water spider is very busy today. She is planning to spin a web underwater. She cannot breathe underwater like a fish, so she is taking a bubble of air with her. She is holding it close to her
10 body while she swims down under the water. There are other small air bubbles in the hair on her body.

Now she is spinning her web. The web has the shape of a **bell**. Now the web is finished, but the work is not finished **yet**. She is **filling** the web with
15 air bubbles. At the same time she is pushing out all the water. Soon she has a dry silk nest. She makes it very well. No water can **enter** the bell-shaped web. The spider can live on the air in the bubbles for several months.

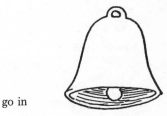

go in

20 The water spider will spend most of her life here. She will eat, sleep, and raise her family.

This strange spider lives only in Europe and parts of Asia. It is the only spider in the world that lives most of its life underwater.

A. Vocabulary

spider	legs	filling	holding
enter	bell-shaped	yet	web
silk	bell	spins	shapes

1. It _____ a _____ with _____ from its body.
2. No water can _____ the bell-shaped web.
3. A _____ is like an insect, but it has eight legs and two parts to its body.
4. The web has the shape of a _____ .
5. Different spiders make webs with different _____ .
6. Now the web is finished, but the work is not finished _____ .
7. She is _____ the web with air bubbles.

B. Vocabulary (new context)

bell	spiders	enter	shape
spinning	raise	bell-shaped	silk
bubbles	fill	web	yet

1. It is summer, so we are going to _____ the swimming pool with water.
2. You can _____ the building through either the front or the side door.
3. Some people are afraid of _____ , but most spiders are not dangerous.
4. A circle is one _____ . A square is another.
5. The _____ rings every hour on the hour. Then it is time for classes to begin.
6. A spider catches insects in its _____ .
7. Are you finished with my dictionary? No, not _____ .
8. Leila has a beautiful new _____ dress.
9. Each dancer is _____ around in a circle.

C. Vocabulary Review

dirty	tools	island	reach
over	lying	coast	sunset
Rocky	strong	lower	hang
lazy	toenails	at all	temperature

1. What is the _____ in the winter in your country? Is it cold?
2. Some women paint their _____ red.
3. Tony put all his _____ clothes in the washer, added some soap, and turned it on.
4. Ali is _____ . He doesn't like to do his homework.
5. Japan is an _____ country.
6. Children's school desks are _____ than adults' desks.
7. The _____ Mountains are in the western United States.
8. Keiko is _____ on the sofa. She is very tired.
9. The _____ last night was very beautiful. The western sky was all different colors.
10. Cape Verde is off the west _____ of Africa.
11. I don't have any money _____ with me. I forgot to bring any.
12. A mechanic uses one kind of _____ . A carpenter uses a different kind because he works with wood.

D. Questions

*1. How many legs does an insect have and how many parts to its body?
2. Describe a spider.
3. What do we call a spider's nest?
4. How does a spider make one?
5. Can a spider breathe water like a fish?
6. What is the water spider doing today?
7. What is she taking underwater with her?
8. How is she carrying it?
9. What shape does her web have?
10. What is she doing with the water in the web?
11. How long can the spider live on the air bubbles?
12. Where will she spend most of her life?
13. How is the water spider different from other spiders?
*14. How is a water spider like a dolphin?

E. Comprehension: True/False/No Information

_____ 1. An insect has six legs.
_____ 2. A spider spins a web.
_____ 3. Spider webs are all alike.
_____ 4. Some spiders can breathe water.
_____ 5. A water spider has a hairy body.
_____ 6. A water spider spins a web underwater.
_____ 7. Every few weeks, the spider has to work on her web again.
_____ 8. No water can enter the nest.
_____ 9. The water spider leaves her nest sometimes to look for food.
_____ 10. Water spiders live in Africa.
_____ 11. There are two kinds of spiders that live underwater.

F. Main Idea

1. The water spider is unusual because it lives underwater.
2. A water spider fills her web with air bubbles and pushes out the water.
3. An insect and a spider are not alike.

WORD STUDY

A. Present Continuous Tense

Use the present continuous for something that is happening right now. Use **am, is,** or **are** and the **-ing** form of the verb (**be + V-ing**).

Example: Now she **is spinning** her web.
             The arctic terns **are flying** toward the south.

Spelling: 1. Use the **1-1-1** rule (see p. 24).
               spin – spinning   put – putting

           2. If the verb ends in **e**, drop the **e** and add **ing**.
               live – living   leave – leaving

           3. If the verb ends in **ie**, change the **ie** to **y**.
               lie – lying   die – dying

           4. If the verb ends in **y**, don't make any changes.
               study – studying   fly – flying

Write sentences in the present continuous tense. Tell something that is happening now. Use these verbs.

1.	dig	6.	study
2.	jump	7.	lie
3.	sit	8.	fry
4.	work	9.	use
5.	plan	10.	carry

B. Irregular Verbs

1. Memorize these verb forms. Then use the past tense of each verb in a sentence.

Simple	**Past**	**Simple**	**Past**
a. become	became	e. win	won
b. buy	bought	f. find	found
c. fight	fought	g. put	put
d. bring	brought	h. cut	cut

2. Write the past tense of these verbs:

a. see	h. sell
b. go	i. get
c. be	j. come
d. give	k. grow
e. make	l. teach
f. eat	m. take
g. think	

C. Un-
Un- means **not**.

Add **un** to each of these words. Then put the words in the blanks.

happy	popular	like	cover
hurt	afraid	kind	common

1. A water spider is _____ . It lives only in Europe and parts of Asia.
2. Tom is often _____ to people, so he is _____ . People don't like him because he is not nice to them.
3. Carol is only fourteen years old. She was alone in the house during a storm but she was _____ .
4. The baby fell off a chair but she was _____ .

D. Compound Words
Put a word from Column A with a word from Column B and make a compound word. Write it in Column C.

Column A	Column B	Column C
1. under	a. light	_____
2. under	b. mate	_____
3. sun	c. work	_____
4. sun	d. water	_____
5. spring	e. food	_____
6. near	f. not	_____

7.	room	g. by
8.	sea	h. time
9.	home	i. line
10.	can	j. rise

_____
_____
_____
_____

E. Context Clues

1. Keiko has $100. Betty has $75. Betty has **less** money than Keiko.
   a. more
   b. the same as
   c. not as much
   d. a lot of

2. There are hundreds of square kilometers of **forests** in the Amazon River area. There are trees everywhere.
   a. lots of trees
   b. some trees
   c. lots of water
   d. some water

3. The Browns are planning to **take a trip** to Florida this summer.
   a. fall down
   b. travel
   c. buy something
   d. give something

4. Beginning students know only **a few** English words. Advanced students know a lot.
   a. not very many
   b. quickly
   c. many
   d. alone

5. Children start to **attend** school when they are five or six years old.
   a. finish
   b. solve
   c. go to
   d. hang on

6. Eskimos **hunt** the polar bear. When they find one, they kill it.
   a. look for and kill
   b. study
   c. hurt
   d. appear

7. What is your **age**? Are you twenty years old yet?
   a. How tall are you?
   b. Where are you from?
   c. How much do you weigh?
   d. How old are you?

8. **Perhaps** there will be large guayule farms some day.
   a. over
   b. maybe
   c. below
   d. at all

9. I was in California for a year but I did **not ever** visit San Diego. I was too busy to go there.
   a. never
   b. possibly
   c. probably
   d. suddenly

10. We must **somehow** stop using so much energy or we will use all of our petroleum.
    a. somebody
    b. in some place
    c. nobody
    d. in some way

11. When did you **arrive** at this university? Did you come here in September?
    a. come
    b. alone
    c. leave
    d. hold on

12. Kenya was a British **colony**. Mexico was a Spanish **colony**. Algeria was a French **colony**.
    a. large coffee farm
    b. international company
    c. farming area
    d. place or country that belongs to another country

Unit VI

INTERESTING PEOPLE OF THE WORLD

THE LAPPS OF NORTHERN EUROPE

1

The Lapps live in northern Norway, Sweden, Finland, and the Soviet Union. There are only about 32,000 of them, and most of them live a modern life on the coast or in the **forests**. Only a
5 few of them live a **traditional** life. These few mountain Lapps are called **nomads** because they move from one place to another with their **reindeer**. Their life is almost the same as it was a thousand years ago.

area with lots of trees

10 In winter the reindeer dig through the snow to find plants for their food. In spring these plants become very dry, and there are lots of insects. Then the Lapps move their reindeer to the coast. The deer live on the thick grass there until winter.
15 When the snow becomes **deep**, the Lapps and their reindeer begin moving slowly back to their winter homes. There is **less** snow there.

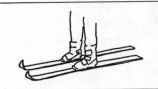

not much

These nomads live in **tents** because they move so often. They make shoes, jackets, and
20 pants of reindeer skin. They also wear beautiful blue and red traditional clothes. They walk or travel on **skis**. They have **sleds** too. Reindeer pull the sleds.

The long **trips**, often in stormy weather,
25 make life very hard for these nomads. More and

more people are staying in villages on the coast. Sometimes a mother and her children travel by car and meet the father in their winter home.

30   There will probably be no more Lapp nomads in the **future**. People want a **comfortable** life. However, the Lapps will probably always wear their traditional clothes on holidays. They will teach their children the old stories and songs. People do not want to forget their traditions.

A. Vocabulary

traditional	winter	trips	comfortable
clothes	forests	deep	skis
few	reindeer	blue	tents
future	sleds	nomads	less

1. Only a few of them live a _____ life.
2. There will probably be no more Lapp nomads in the _____ .
3. When the snow becomes_____ , the Lapps and their reindeer begin moving slowly back to their winter homes.
4. There are only about 32,000 of them, and most of them live a modern life on the coast or in the _____ .
5. People want a _____ life.
6. These few mountain Lapps are called _____ because they move from one place to another with their _____ .
7. The long_____ , often in stormy weather, make life very hard for these nomads.
8. They have _____ too.
9. They walk or travel on _____ .
10. There is _____ snow there.
11. These nomads live in _____ because they move so often.

INTERESTING PEOPLE

B. Vocabulary (new context)

forests	trip	traditional	stormy
tent	future	few	ski
nomads	slowly	comfortable	sleds
another	deep	stories	less

1. Helen and Tom are going to take a _____ to England next year.
2. Eastern Canada has large _____ . There are millions of trees.
3. The water in the Pacific Ocean is very _____ .
4. In northern countries, children like to play on their _____ in winter. They also like to _____ .
5. The Baker family likes to go camping. They sleep in a _____ .
6. _____ in the Sahara Desert travel with their camels.
7. What are your plans for the _____ ? What are you going to do?
8. Most people in Saudi Arabia dress in _____ clothes. A few people wear western clothes.
9. This chair is not very _____ . It is too hard.
10. Twelve is _____ than fifteen.

C. Vocabulary Review
Match the words that mean the same.

Column A
1. pass _____
2. terrible _____
3. below _____
4. alone _____
5. storm _____
6. over _____
7. quickly _____
8. web _____
9. adult _____
10. island _____

Column B
a. fill
b. go or move
c. land with water all around it
d. under
e. shape
f. very bad
g. with no light
h. not with anyone
i. above
j. a spider's nest
k. man or woman
l. fast
m. bad weather

D. Questions

1. In what countries do the Lapps live?
2. Do they all move from one place to another?
3. What are nomads?
4. Does the life of Lapp nomads change very much?
5. How do reindeer find their food in winter?
6. Why do these Lapps move away from the coast in winter?
7. Why do they live in tents?
8. How do they travel?
9. What makes life hard for these nomads?
10. Why will these Lapps probably change their lives?
*11. Where do other nomads live?
12. Why will the Lapps teach their children the old songs and stories?
*13. Why do people want to keep their traditions?
*14. Are there roads in northern Scandinavia?

E. Comprehension: True/False

_____ 1. There are Lapps in Russia.
_____ 2. Only a few Lapps are nomads.
_____ 3. Lapp nomads raise sheep and goats.
_____ 4. Most Lapps live in large cities.
_____ 5. Reindeer find their food on trees.
_____ 6. Lapp nomads spend the summer on the coast.
_____ *7. Lapp nomads probably eat reindeer meat.
_____ *8. They carry their tents on sleds.
_____ 9. Traveling in stormy weather is difficult.
_____ *10. Nomads in other countries probably want to keep their traditions and have a comfortable life too.

F. Main Idea

1. A few Lapps live a traditional life but that life is difficult.
2. Lapp nomads move their reindeer every summer and winter.
3. Lapps want to keep some of their traditions.

THE AINU OF JAPAN

2

The Ainu live in northern Japan on the island of Hokkaido. They do not look like other Japanese. They have round, dark brown eyes and **wavy** hair. The men have **beards** and **mustaches**. Where did
5 these people come from? Did they come from Europe **across** Russia to Japan? Did they come from Indonesia? Are they **completely** different from all the other people in the world? Nobody knows the answers to these questions.

10 The Ainu were in Japan 7,000 years ago. In modern times, the Japanese brought new diseases to Ainu villages. Many people died. Today there are only 300 Ainu **left**. There are also about a thousand people who are part Ainu.

15 The Ainu eat seafood and grow rice and vegetables on their farms. The men **hunt** for brown bears in the forests. They eat the meat and sell the skins. The bear is also important in their religion.

People make their houses from a kind of
20 grass. There is only one room inside. It has a dirt floor with an open fire in the **middle**. Their religion tells them that the house must have one window on the east side.

Young Ainu **attend** school with other Jap-
25 anese. They speak Japanese and don't know their own language. They want to be like other young Japanese.

straight hair

100% wavy hair

curly hair

mustache

beard

go to

The Lapps in northern Europe want to **continue** their traditions. Young Ainu don't want to
30 learn their traditions. When the old people die, the Ainu traditions will die with them.

A. Vocabulary

round	completely	middle	continue
attend	mustaches	wavy	bear
across	beards	hunt	left

1. Did they come from Europe _____ Russia to Japan?
2. Today there are only 300 Ainu _____ .
3. Young Ainu _____ school with other Japanese.
4. The men have _____ and _____ .
5. The men _____ for brown bears in the forests.
6. They have round, dark brown eyes and _____ hair.
7. It has a dirt floor with an open fire in the _____ .
8. Are they _____ different from all the other people in the world?
9. The Lapps in northern Europe want to _____ their traditions.

B. Vocabulary (new context)

continue	attend	mustache	sell
wavy	middle	completely	beard
brown	across	hunting	left

1. We ate all the bananas. There aren't any _____ .
2. The students _____ finished the book. They did every page.
3. Number 4 is in the _____ of this exercise.
4. Carlos has _____ brown hair. He has a _____ and a _____ too.
5. Where did you _____ high school?

6. _____ is a popular sport in some countries.
7. Sarah walked _____ the street to the bank.
8. We did not have time to finish the lesson. We will _____ it tomorrow.

C. Vocabulary Review

hold on	upside down	suddenly	enough
appeared	area	solve	yet
silk	entered	bells	mixture
roast	invented	ears	hole

1. The number 6 is like a 9 but it is _____ .
2. Water in a river cannot move when it is covered with water hyacinths. Scientists are trying to _____ this problem.
3. Superman suddenly _____ from the sky.
4. Thomas Edison _____ the electric light.
5. The sloth does not have _____ energy to move fast.
6. Coke is a _____ of cola flavor, water, carbon dioxide, and sugar.
7. Oscar _____ the class a week late.
8. Many Americans have _____ beef for Sunday dinner.
9. Some church _____ sound beautiful.
10. My toenail made a _____ in my sock.
11. Little children _____ to their mother's hands when they walk across the street.
12. Did your cousin pass the TOEFL test _____ ?

D. Questions

1. Where do the Ainu live?
2. What do they look like?
3. Where did they come from?
4. How many Ainu are there today?
*5. What will happen to the Ainu people if most of the children marry other Japanese?

6. Why do Ainu men hunt brown bears?
7. Describe a traditional Ainu house.
8. What language do young Ainu speak?
*9. Why do young Ainu want to be like other Japanese?
10. What will happen to Ainu traditions if the young people don't learn them?

E. Comprehension

1. Ainu have _____ eyes.
   a. green
   b. black
   c. blue
   d. brown

2. Ainu are different from other Japanese because _____ .
   a. they have hair
   b. they have beards
   c. they have mustaches
   d. they have round eyes

3. Today there are only _____ Ainu left.
   a. 300
   b. 1,000
   c. 10,000
   d. 7,000

*4. Ainu and other Japanese are alike because _____ .
   a. they have grass houses
   b. they have wavy hair
   c. they hunt bears
   d. they eat seafood and rice

5. The Ainu house has a window on the east side _____ .
   a. to let in sunlight
   b. because of their religion
   c. to look at the mountains
   d. to look for bears

6. Young Ainu speak _____ .
   a. only Ainu
   b. only Japanese
   c. Ainu and Japanese
   d. English

7. Young Ainu attend _____ .
   a. Ainu schools
   b. Japanese dances
   c. Japanese schools
   d. soccer games

F. Main Idea

Put the letter of the supporting details under the correct main ideas. Two of the details do not belong under a main idea.

1. How an Ainu looks   2. An Ainu's house   3. Young Ainu

    a. The men have mustaches.
    b. They speak only Japanese.
    c. They want to keep their traditions.
    d. There is an open fire in the middle.
    e. They were in Japan 7,000 years ago.
    f. They have round eyes.
    g. There is a dirt floor.
    h. They don't want to learn the traditions.
    i. They have wavy hair.
    j. It is made of a kind of grass.
    k. It has a window on the east side.
    l. The men have beards

THE TASADAYS
OF THE PHILIPPINES

3

In 1971 the world learned about the Tasaday people. They live on the island of Mindanao in the Philippines. A hunter found them and took a government **official** to visit them.

important government worker

5 The Tasadays live in the tropical forest. They live in **caves** in the mountains far away from other people. There are only 24 of them. They knew nothing about other people on Mindanao, about Manila, the government, or modern life. They lived
10 in their own world.

The Tasadays were Stone **Age** people. They used stone tools. They had no **metal**. They had stone **axes** for cutting. They used digging **sticks** and **bamboo** knives. They used two sticks to make
15 a fire. They never hunted animals and they had no farms. They wore a few leaves for clothes. They ate insects, **frogs**, fish, wild fruit, and leaves.

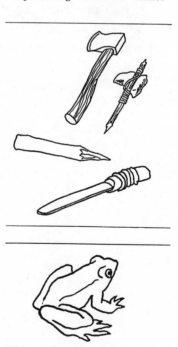

Now their lives are changing very fast. Other mountain people are teaching them to eat different
20 kinds of food. People are giving them metal knives and other tools. They have **cloth** now. It keeps them warm during the cool nights. Every time they get something new, they want more modern things.

INTERESTING PEOPLE

The Tasadays are learning many new things
25 from the rest of the world. They can teach us
something too. They have no word for war or hate
or enemy. They never kill anyone. They never **hit**
their children. <u>**Perhaps**</u> they have something   maybe
more important to teach than to learn.

A. Vocabulary

frogs	official	sticks	perhaps
cloth	hit	caves	knives
bamboo	axes	metal	Age

1. They live in _____ in the mountains far away from other people.
2. They ate insects, _____ , fish, wild fruit, and leaves.
3. A hunter found them and took a government _____ to visit them.
4. They had stone _____ for cutting.
5. They never _____ their children.
6. They used digging_____ and_____ knives.
7. _____ they have something more important to teach than to learn.
8. They had no _____ .
9. The Tasadays were Stone _____ people.
10. They have _____ now.

B. Vocabulary (new context)

age	caves	perhaps	metal
official	sticks	frog	axe
cloth	knives	hit	visit

1. People make clothes out of _____ .
2. Some _____ are very beautiful inside.
3. A _____ lives in the water but it cannot breathe underwater.
4. When were you born? What is your _____ ?
5. Ali isn't in class today. _____ he is sick.
6. Nadia's father is a government _____ . He works in the Ministry of Education.
7. Some desks are wooden. Some are _____ .
8. Some birds build a nest out of small _____ .
9. The baseball player _____ the ball and ran around the bases.
10. Oscar cut down a tree with an _____ .

C. Vocabulary Review
Match the words that mean the opposite.

Column A
1. higher _____
2. cleaner _____
3. child _____
4. began _____
5. over _____
6. wet _____
7. upside down _____
8. more _____
9. future _____
10. alone _____
11. a few _____
12. terrible _____

Column B
a. right side up
b. across
c. a lot
d. lower
e. stopped
f. together
g. wonderful
h. under
i. middle
j. past
k. dirtier
l. less
m. adult
n. dry

D. Questions

*1. How long ago did the world learn about the Tasadays?
2. In what country do they live?
3. Where are their caves?
*4. What are Stone Age people?
*5. Why didn't the Tasadays know about other people?
6. Describe their tools.
7. How did they make a fire?
8. What did they eat?
9. Name some changes in their lives.
10. What words are not in their language?
11. What can the Tasadays teach us?
*12. What do you think will happen to the Tasadays? Why?

E. Comprehension: True/False/No Information

_____ 1. The Tasadays live in a tropical forest.
_____ 2. The Philippine government wants to take care of the Tasadays.
_____ 3. Today the Tasadays have radios.
_____ 4. They visited other villages to buy food.
_____ 5. We call them Stone Age people because they used stone tools.
_____ 6. They hunted with stone axes.
_____ 7. They made a fire with two sticks.
_____ 8. They had small farms near their caves.
_____ 9. The Tasadays are afraid of new things.
_____ 10. Now the Tasadays visit other villages.
_____ 11. We could learn something from them.

F. Main Idea

1. The Tasadays were Stone Age people but now their lives are changing very fast.
2. The Tasadays live in the tropical forest in the Philippines but they know nothing about other Filipinos.
3. The Tasadays never hit their children and never kill anyone.

THE HOPI INDIANS OF ARIZONA

The Hopi Indians live in the northeastern part of Arizona in the United States. The United States is a very modern country. Tall buildings, highways, **computers**, and hundreds of other
5 modern things are a part of every American's life. **Somehow**, with modern things all around them, the Hopis keep their traditions.

in some way

There are about 5,000 Hopis and they live in thirteen villages in the desert. The weather is very
10 hot in summer, but in winter it **freezes**. Farming is difficult.

goes below 0° C.

Corn is the Hopis' main food, but they plant vegetables too. They raise sheep, goats, and **cattle**. They also eat hamburgers and ice cream and drink
15 soft drinks. They live in traditional stone houses, but many of them have telephones, radios, and television. They have horses but they have **pickup trucks** too.

cows

Kachinas are an important part of the Hopi
20 religion. Kachinas are **spirits** of **dead** people, of rocks, plants, and animals, and of the stars. Men dress as kachinas and do religious dances. People also make wooden kachina dolls. No two wooden kachinas are **ever** alike.

dead = adjective for *die*

not ever = never

25   The children attend school and learn English
and other subjects. A few Hopis go to university.
Some of the adults live and work in nearby towns.
The children attend school, but they also learn the
Hopi language, dances, and stories. The Hopis
30 want a comfortable modern life, but they don't
want to **lose** their traditions.   verb for *lost*

A. Vocabulary

somehow	ever	rocks	lose
computers	goats	kachinas	dead
freezes	pickup trucks	cattle	spirits

1. Tall buildings, highways, _____ , and hundreds of other modern things are a part of every American's life.
2. They have horses, but they have _____ too.
3. _____ are an important part of the Hopi religion.
4. The Hopis want a comfortable, modern life, but they don't want to _____ their traditions.
5. _____ , with modern things all around them, the Hopis keep their traditions.
6. Kachinas are _____ of _____ people, of rocks, plants, and animals, and of the stars.
7. No two wooden kachinas are _____ alike.
8. They raise sheep, goats, and _____ .
9. The weather is very hot in summer but in winter it _____ .

B. Vocabulary (new context)

pickup	dead	lose	computer
somehow	television	freezes	spirits
nearby	cattle	ever	religious

1. Terns _____ find their way from Antarctica to the Arctic every year.
2. Some African villagers say that trees and rocks have _____ .
3. Beef comes from _____ .
4. Most cowboys have a _____ truck and a horse.
5. The cashiers in modern supermarkets use a _____ .
6. President John F. Kennedy died in 1963. He is _____ .
7. Water _____ at 0° C and changes into ice.
8. A sloth cannot _____ move fast. It always moves slowly.
9. Did you _____ your new pen? Is it lost?

C. Vocabulary Review

deep	skiing	trip	nomads
tent	sled	uncomfortable	wavy
attend	beard	complete	continues
cards	dark	reach	set

1. Russians traveled by _____ in winter before they had cars and buses.
2. Let's play a game of _____ . I don't feel like studying.
3. Riding for hours on a motorcycle is _____ .
4. David's parents took a _____ to South America last year.
5. The Mississippi River is very _____ in some places.
6. _____ in Central Asia take their sheep into the mountains in summer.
7. Are you planning to _____ the dance next Saturday?
8. The story on some television programs _____ from one week to the next.
9. Ruth and Ann are going camping in the mountains. They have a _____ to sleep in.

10. Oscar didn't have time to _____ his composition before the bell rang.
11. Howard has _____ blond hair and a short _____ .
12. Did you ever go _____ in Switzerland in the winter?

D. Questions

1. Where do the Hopis live?
2. What things are a part of every American's life?
3. What is the weather like in the Hopi villages?
4. What is their main food?
*5. What kind of meat do they eat?
6. Do they eat food that other Americans eat?
7. What is modern about some of their homes? What is traditional?
8. Where do the children learn English?
9. What are kachinas?
10. Why do they teach their children the language, dances, and stories?
*11. Are Hopi children more like Lapp or Ainu children? Why?

E. Comprehension

1. Hopis live in the state of _____ .
   a. Utah
   b. New Mexico
   c. Arizona
   d. New York

2. Hopis _____ .
   a. want modern things instead of traditional ones
   b. want traditional things instead of modern ones
   c. don't want to remember their traditions
   d. want both modern and traditional things

3. Winters in this part of Arizona are _____ .
   a. hot
   b. warm
   c. cool
   d. cold

4. The main Hopi food is _____ .
   a. corn
   b. hamburgers
   c. beef
   d. vegetables

*5. A pickup truck is useful for people _____ .
   a. in a city apartment
   b. on a farm
   c. in New York City
   d. near an airport

*6. Hopis probably eat _____ sometimes.
   a. frogs
   b. polar bears
   c. potato chips and pizza
   d. reindeer meat

7. Kachinas are _____ .
   a. men
   b. something to eat
   c. animals
   d. spirits

8. Hopis don't want to _____ their traditions.
   a. lose
   b. hit
   c. remember
   d. learn

F. Main Idea

1. Hopis raise crops and animals in the Arizona desert.
2. Kachinas are spirits of the things around the Hopis.
3. Hopis keep their traditions even with modern life all around them.

THE MAORIS
OF NEW ZEALAND

5

Polynesians live on islands in the Pacific Ocean. The Maoris are Polynesians and they live at the southern end of Polynesia in New Zealand. There are about 280,000 Maoris today.

5   Maoris, like other Polynesians, have brown skin, dark brown eyes, and wavy black hair. Men have beards and mustaches, but they usually **shave** them.

The Maoris **arrived** in New Zealand from
10 other Polynesian islands **over** a thousand years ago. They were the first people to live there. They made beautiful wooden buildings with pictures cut into the wood.

came
more than

There was one terrible thing about their life.
15 They fought wars **among themselves** for several centuries. However, in 1840 they **agreed** to become a British **colony** to bring peace to the country. When they stopped fighting, they learned European ways quickly.

between

20 Today there are Maoris in all kinds of jobs. They attend school and university and become lawyers and scientists. There are Maoris in the government. Most of them live like white New Zealanders.

25   However, the Maoris do not forget their traditions. Children learn the language, music, and old stories. They have **yearly competitions** in   every year speaking, dancing, and singing. They **practice** for months. Then all the Maoris in the area arrive to
30 watch the competitions and see old friends. Most of the time Maoris live a comfortable modern life. They spend part of the time passing on their traditions to their children.

A. Vocabulary

among	islands	yearly	over
wavy	competitions	arrived	themselves
practice	colony	shave	agreed

1. The Maoris _____ in New Zealand from other Polynesian islands _____ a thousand years ago.
2. They have_____ _____ in speaking, dancing, and singing.
3. Men have beards and mustaches, but they usually _____ them.
4. They fought wars _____ _____ for several centuries.
5. However, in 1840 they _____ to become a British _____ to bring peace to the country.
6. They _____ for months.

B. Vocabulary (new context)

arrive	yearly	practice	music
competition	themselves	colony	over
shave	among	agree	passing

1. The children made lunch_____ because their parents weren't home.

2. You should _____ your English outside of class. Speak English _____ yourselves between classes.
3. There is a sports _____ this week. Students from six universities are coming.
4. I think that the Lapp nomads have a very hard life. Do you _____ ?
5. What time does your plane _____ in Chicago?
6. Some men have to _____ every day.
7. Brazil was a Portuguese _____ .
8. English teachers go to a _____ meeting. They go every year.
9. The Ainu arrived in Japan _____ 7,000 years ago.

C. Vocabulary Review
Match the words that mean the same.

Column A
1. not ever _____
2. freeze _____
3. perhaps _____
4. dead _____
5. less _____
6. attend _____
7. somehow _____
8. travel _____
9. thick _____
10. desert _____

Column B
a. not alive
b. in some way
c. a dry area
d. never
e. take a trip
f. fewer
g. change to ice
h. computer
i. spirit
j. go to
k. not thin
l. maybe

D. Questions

1. Where do Polynesians live?
*2. Where is New Zealand?
3. How many Maoris are there?
4. What do Maoris look like?
5. Where did the Maoris come from?
6. What was terrible about their life?
7. Why did they agree to become a British colony?

8. Do Maoris attend university?
9. How do most Maoris live today?
10. What do they do at their yearly competitions?
*11. How are the Maoris, Ainu, and Tasadays alike?

E. Comprehension: True/False

_____ *1. Today Maoris probably wear their traditional clothing.
_____   2. Maoris are Polynesians.
_____   3. New Zealand is an island country.
_____   4. Maoris look like Chinese.
_____   5. When the Maoris arrived in New Zealand, they fought with the other people there.
_____   6. The Maoris wanted peace in their country.
_____   7. Maoris live by hunting and fishing.
_____ *8. There are probably Maori teachers.
_____   9. Maoris like music.
_____ *10. Maoris teach their children to fight wars against the white people.

F. Main Idea
Write the numbers of the supporting ideas under the right names. Some may go under more than one name.

Lapps   Ainu   Tasadays   Hopis   Maoris

1. They live on an island.
2. They live in a cave.
3. They live in a grass house with a dirt floor.
4. They have stone houses.
5. They live part of the year in tents.
6. They were the first people on their island.
7. They had only stone tools.
8. Corn is their main food.

9. They eat reindeer meat.
10. They have farms.
11. They live in the desert.
12. They live in the far north.
13. There are only a few of them left.
14. They need warm clothes.
15. They have no words for war, hate, or enemy.
16. Their traditions will probably die.

WORD STUDY

A. -self Pronouns (Reflexive Pronouns)
A mirror **reflects. Reflexive** pronouns reflect on the subject of the sentence.

Example: **You** see **yourself** in the mirror.
The Maoris fought wars among **themselves.**
I don't need any help. **I** can do it **myself.**

Subject Pronoun	Reflexive Pronoun
I	myself
you	yourself
he	himself
she	herself
it	itself
we	ourselves
you	yourselves
they	themselves

Put the right **-self** pronoun in the blanks.

1.   We usually speak English among _____ at the Student Union.
2.   No one can practice English for you. You have to do it_____ .
3.   You should practice among _____ .
4.   The officials agreed among _____ .
5.   A modern elevator moves by_____ when someone pushes the button.
6.   The water spider holds an air bubble against_____ while she swims down under the water.
7.   No one told me about it. I saw it _____ .
8.   Carlos taught _____ how to speak English.

B. Superlatives
When we compare two things or people, we use the comparative forms **-er, more, better, worse,** or **farther than.**

INTERESTING PEOPLE

When we compare three or more things or people, we use **the** + adjective + **est** with words of one syllable.

Example: Tom is **the oldest** student in the class.

We use **the most** + adjective with words of three or more syllables.

Example: Ann is **the most intelligent** student in the class.

Irregular: good – better than – the best
            bad – worse than   – the worst
            far   – farther than – the farthest

Example: Ann is **the best** student in the class.
            Sarah is **the worst** student in the class.
            Mary ran **the farthest**.

Spelling: Use the **1-1-1** rule (see p. 24).

big – biggest

Put the superlative form of the adjective in the blank. Use **the**.

(beautiful)   1. Switzerland is _____ country in Europe.

(expensive)   2. A Rolls Royce is _____ kind of car in the world.

(good)   3. This morning Kumiko wrote _____ composition that she ever wrote.

(tall)   4. Who is _____ student in the class?

(important)   5. Rice is _____ food for millions of people.

(far)   6. Who drives _____ to come to class?

(bad)   7. Teachers think that bubble gum is _____ kind of gum.

(dark)   8. Black is _____ color.

(strong)   9. Who is _____ person in your family?

C. Word Forms

	Verb	Noun	Adjective
1.	use	use	useful
2.		tropics	tropical
3.	sweeten	sweetener	sweet
4.	mix	mixture	
5.	weigh	weight	
6.	fill		full
7.		tradition	traditional
8.		wood	wooden
9.		religion	religious
10.		noise	noisy

Put the right word form in each blank. Choose a word form from line 1 for sentence 1. Choose a word form from line 2 for sentence 2, and so on.

1. A metal knife is very _____ for the Tasadays.
2. Northern Brazil is a _____ area.
3. You can _____ your tea with some sugar.
4. An ice cream soda is a _____ of ice cream and a soft drink.
5. What is the _____ of an arctic tern?
6. His coffee cup is _____ .
7. Music is an important Maori _____ .
8. Hopis do not live in _____ houses.
9. What is your _____ ?
10. Some children are very _____ .

D. Irregular Verbs

1. Memorize these verb forms. Then use the past tense of each verb in a sentence.

Simple	Past	Simple	Past
a. do	did	e. blow	blew
b. have	had	f. know	knew
c. ring	rang	g. hit	hit
d. begin	began	h. tell	told

2. Write the past tense of these verbs.

a. become   g. fight
b. buy   h. go
c. bring   i. get
d. cut   j. see
e. come   k. teach
f. find   l. win

E. Context Clues

1. Captain James Cook was a famous English **explorer**. He was the first European to visit most of the Pacific islands.
   a. a place that has water all around it
   b. a businessman who travels to different countries
   c. a person who looks for new places and information about them
   d. a ship that travels to new places

2. Captain Cook's ship had **sailors** on it, because there is a lot of work on a ship.
   a. men who do the work on a ship
   b. men who live in colonies
   c. people in competitions
   d. people who travel on ships during their vacation

3. There **might** be a quiz on Friday. If we don't finish the lesson Thursday, the quiz will be Monday.
   a. will   c. perhaps will
   b. is going to   d. was

4. Ruth had to study the **history** of Europe in school. She learned about wars, kings, governments, religion, and many other things.
   a. the mountains, rivers, and lakes
   b. the countries, cities, and towns
   c. scientists and the things they invent
   d. everything that happened in the past

5. Abdullah always gets good grades on his tests so **I suppose** he will get a good grade on this one too.
   a. think   c. want
   b. dinner   d. have to

6. Helen's family and friends had a party and gave her **gifts** on her twenty-first birthday.
    a. $100
    b. presents
    c. food
    d. cattle

7. Helen was very **pleased** when she saw the gifts.
    a. unhappy
    b. deep
    c. afraid
    d. happy

8. A hippopotamus is **heavy**. A spider is not **heavy**.
    a. deep
    b. very tall
    c. weighs a lot
    d. has six legs

9. Masako was playing basketball and she **injured** her arm. She went to the doctor and cannot play again for six months.
    a. hurt
    b. told
    c. arrived
    d. won

10. Masako's arm is better now. She is **glad** that she can play basketball again.
    a. hurt
    b. dead
    c. happy
    d. jump

11. I found a writing book, but it has no name in it. Who does it **belong to**?
    a. Where is it?
    b. Whose is it?
    c. What is it?
    d. When is it?

12. Dan is three years old. He is **able to** walk and talk, but he can't read or write.
    a. can
    b. has to
    c. wants to
    d. plans to

13. This television program is one hour long. It starts at 8:00 and is **over** at 9:00.
    a. wonderful
    b. double
    c. finished
    d. middle

14. The Amazon River area is in the tropics. Many kinds of animals live in the **jungle** there.
    a. desert
    b. tropical forest
    c. ice and snow
    d. towns

Unit VII

EXPLORATION AND ADVENTURE

THE POLYNESIANS

1

The Polynesians were probably the best **explorers** in the **history** of the world. They traveled thousands of kilometers across the Pacific Ocean in large **double canoes**. They could look at
5 the stars and know which way to go. They also understood the wind and ocean **currents**. They made **maps** of the stars and ocean currents. They made these maps out of sticks and **shells**.

About four thousand years ago a group of
10 Polynesians lived in southern China. They were a mixture of white, black, and Mongol people. When the Chinese moved farther and farther into the south, the Polynesians needed to find **safer** homes.

Slowly these Polynesians left China in their
15 double canoes and started toward the southeast. They took animals and plants with them. A group of people **might** arrive at an island and stay there until they had children, grandchildren, and great-grandchildren. Then a few families might start
20 traveling again. Some canoes went one way and some went another. It took hundreds of years for them to reach all of the islands in Polynesia.

The Polynesian double canoe is one of the **greatest** inventions in history. The Polynesians
25 were among the greatest **sailors** in history. They understood how to sail by the stars, wind, and ocean currents. This made them great explorers.

rivers in the ocean

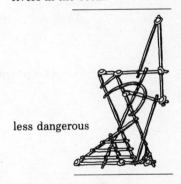

less dangerous

would maybe

best, most wonderful

A. Vocabulary

explorers	safer	history	maps
greatest	grandchildren	sailors	double
shells	canoes	might	currents

1. The Polynesian double canoe is one of the _____ inventions in history.
2. When the Chinese moved farther and farther into the south, the Polynesians needed to find _____ homes.
3. The Polynesians were probably the best _____ in the _____ of the world.
4. A group of people _____ arrive at an island and stay there until they had children, grandchildren, and great-grandchildren.
5. The Polynesians were among the greatest _____ in history.
6. They also understood the wind and ocean _____ .
7. They traveled thousands of miles across the Pacific Ocean in large _____ _____ .
8. They made _____ of the stars and ocean currents.
9. They made these maps out of sticks and _____ .

B. Vocabulary (new context)

southeast	shell	might	history
safe	great	double	map
sailor	explorer	current	canoe

1. Madame Curie was a _____ scientist.
2. Children study the _____ of their country.
3. We _____ go to Los Angeles for our vacation but we are not sure.
4. A warm ocean _____ off the coast of Norway makes Norway warmer than Sweden.
5. A _____ works on a ship.
6. Can you find Polynesia on the _____ ?
7. It isn't _____ for little children to play alone in a swimming pool.
8. A _____ is a small sea animal's house.

9. If you _____ three, you get six.
10. Marco Polo was a great Italian _____ . He crossed Asia and
    lived in China for several years in the thirteenth century.
11. Some North American Indians traveled by _____ .

C. Vocabulary Review

ground	hang	fur	lazy
temperature	jumped	enough	shape
yet	silk	enter	bell
Age	official	metal	frog

1. You should _____ your new silk dress on a hanger in the
    closet.
2. The students are sitting in a circle on the _____ under a tree.
3. You don't have _____ time to have lunch before your next
    class.
4. Did the 10:00 o'clock _____ ring _____ ? I
    didn't hear it.
5. The sixteenth century was the _____ of Exploration for
    Europeans.
6. The _____ in New Zealand is lower than in Hawaii.
7. Polynesia is in the _____ of a triangle (Δ).
8. Three frogs _____ into the water.
9. Insects and small plants live in a sloth's _____ .
10. A sloth moves very slowly, but it is not really _____ .
11. Is your nephew going to _____ the sports competition?

D. Questions

1. What did the Polynesians travel in?
2. How did they know which way to go?
3. What did they make their maps from?
4. Where did Polynesians come from in the beginning?
5. Why did they leave China?
6. What did they take with them?
7.. Did they travel different ways across the ocean?

8. How long did it take for them to reach all of Polynesia?
9. What made the Polynesians great explorers?
*10. Are ocean currents important for ships today? Why?
*11. Are the stars important for ships today? Why?

E. Comprehension: True/False/No Information

_____ 1. Hawaiians are Polynesians.
_____ 2. Maoris are Polynesians.
_____ 3. Polynesians came from southern China.
_____ 4. Polynesians are a mixture of different groups of people.
_____ 5. They traveled from one group of islands to another very quickly.
_____ 6. They took dogs with them from China.
_____ 7. Some people died on the way to new islands.
_____ 8. The Polynesian double canoe is a great invention.
_____ 9. The Polynesians were great sailors and explorers.
_____ 10. They made maps on paper.

F. Main Idea

1. The Polynesians left China and became some of the greatest explorers in history.
2. The Polynesians went from China to hundreds of Pacific Islands.
3. The Polynesians invented the double canoe.

A GIRAFFE
IN CENTRAL ASIA

Tamerlane (1336?–1405) was a very strong
Mongol **leader**. He and his soldiers fought until
Tamerlane became the **ruler** of all Central Asia.
Other countries wanted to make friends with
5 Tamerlane. It was safer to be friends than enemies.

    Ambassadors from many countries took
gifts to Tamerlane. They took beautiful cloth,
jewelry, gold (Au), and **silver** (Ag). They often
tried to take something unusual as a gift too.

10   In 1404, near the end of Tamerlane's life, an
Egyptian ambassador arrived in Samarkand. This
was where Tamerlane lived. The ambassador and
his men traveled on horses and camels. They
brought a **giraffe** from Africa as a gift.

15   Egyptian camels and horses were **used to**
walking in the desert. They did it all the time. A
giraffe is not used to the desert. But this giraffe
walked 5,000 kilometers from Cairo to Samarkand.

    We know about the Egyptian ambassador's
20 gift because several people wrote about it. No one
wrote that Tamerlane liked it. However, we
suppose that he was very **pleased** to have this
strange African animal in Central Asia.

presents

suppose = think, guess /
pleased = happy

A. Vocabulary

make friends	used to	leader	suppose
ambassadors	ruler	pleased	silver
jewelry	gifts	gold	giraffe

1. _____ from many countries took _____ to Tamerlane.
2. Egyptian camels and horses were_____ walking in the desert.
3. Tamerlane (1336?–1405) was a very strong Mongol _____ .
4. They took beautiful cloth, _____ , _____ (Au), and _____ (Ag).
5. However, we _____ that he was very_____ to have this strange African animal in Central Asia.
6. He and his soldiers fought until Tamerlane became the_____ of all Central Asia.
7. They brought a _____ from Africa as a gift.

B. Vocabulary (new context)

giraffe	leader	jewelry	soldiers
suppose	gold	ruler	pleased
used to	silver	gifts	ambassador

1. Who is your country's _____ to the United States?
2. A _____ has a very long neck.
3. _____ jewelry is expensive. _____ jewelry is less expensive than gold.
4. Some women like to wear a lot of _____ .
5. Masako is never absent from class but she is not here today. I_____ she is sick.
6. A king is the _____ of a country. He is also the _____ of his people.
7. When Japanese students study in the United States, they can't get _____ the food because it is very strange.
8. Ali got an excellent grade on his quiz. He was _____ .
9. Americans usually get _____ on their birthday.

C. Vocabulary Review
Match the words that mean the opposite.

Column A
1. arrive _____
2. safe _____
3. inside _____
4. rise _____
5. start _____
6. dead _____
7. lose _____
8. higher _____
9. more _____
10. somebody _____

Column B
a. set
b. fewer
c. find
d. leave
e. outside
f. dangerous
g. great
h. lower
i. stop
j. yearly
k. alive
l. nobody

D. Questions

*1. What does the question mark mean in (1336?–1405)?
2. Who was Tamerlane?
3. Why did other countries want to make friends with him?
*4. Why did ambassadors take gifts to Tamerlane?
5. What kind of gifts did they take?
*6. Why did they often try to take something unusual?
7. Who took a giraffe to Tamerlane?
8. How did the giraffe get to Samarkand?
*9. Do you think Tamerlane liked the giraffe? Why?

E. Comprehension

1. Tamerlane was _____ leader.
   a. an Egyptian
   b. a Chinese
   c. a Mongol
   d. an Arab

2. Tamerlane became the ruler of Central Asia because of _____ .
   a. ambassadors
   b. wars
   c. enemies
   d. gifts

3. Other countries wanted to _____ friends with Tamerlane.
   a. make
   c. buy
   b. give
   d. find

4. Ag means _____ .
   a. jewelry
   c. gold
   b. gifts
   d. silver

5. A giraffe was _____ gift.
   a. an unusual
   c. a double
   b. a safe
   d. a dead

6. Giraffes are not _____ walking in the desert.
   a. arrived
   c. used to
   b. bought
   d. wrote

7. Tamerlane was probably _____ to have this unusual animal.
   a. strong
   c. safer
   b. dangerous
   d. pleased

F. Main Idea

1. An Egyptian ambassador took a giraffe to Tamerlane.
2. Tamerlane was a strong Mongol ruler of Central Asia.
3. Ambassadors took beautiful and unusual gifts to Tamerlane.

THE FIRST WOMAN ON MOUNT EVEREST

3

Mount Everest is the highest mountain in the world. It is in the Himalayan Mountains between Nepal and China, and it is 8,900 meters high. Sir Edmund Hillary from New Zealand and Tenzing
5 Norgay from Nepal were the first people ever to climb Mount Everest. They climbed it in 1953. Men from several different countries climbed it after that.

Junko Tabei, a Japanese from Hokkaido, was
10 the first woman to make this difficult climb. A Tokyo newspaper-television company **organized**   planned the climb in 1975. They **chose** fifteen women from mountaineering **clubs** to go to Nepal. The group climbed for several days. Then there was an
15 **avalanche**. The **heavy** ice and snow **injured** ten   hurt of the women. They had to stop climbing. The other five continued.

Only Ms. Tabei **was able** to climb the last 70   could meters. She was standing on top of the world. She
20 was the first woman there.

Ms. Tabei was 35 years old at the time. She is 1 meter 50 centimeters tall and weighs 42 kilograms. She says that she is an **ordinary** housewife. She started climbing mountains in 1960. She climbed
25 every mountain in Japan. Then she climbed Mount

Annapurna, another high mountain in the Himalayas. **Finally** she climbed the world's highest mountain.

30   When she reached the top, she thought, "I'm at the top and I'm **glad** that I'm at the top." Then she climbed back down the mountain.

happy

A. Vocabulary

injured	ordinary	kilograms	finally
heavy	was able	mountaineering	organized
glad	avalanche	chose	clubs

1. They _____ fifteen women from mountaineering

 _____ .

2. Only Ms. Tabei _____ to climb the last 70 meters.
3. _____ she climbed the world's highest mountain.
4. A Tokyo newspaper-television company _____ the climb.
5. She says that she is an _____ housewife.
6. The _____ ice and snow _____ ten of the women.
7. When she reached the top, she thought, "I'm at the top and I'm _____ that I'm at the top."
8. Then there was an _____ .

B. Vocabulary (new context)

highest	injured	finally	organize
able	glad	mountaineering	heavier
ordinary	choose	club	climb

1. The water spider is not an _____ spider. It is very unusual because it lives underwater.
2. Abdullah took the TOEFL test four times. _____ he passed it. He was not _____ to pass it the first three times. He is very _____ that he finally passed it.

3. If you need a new shirt, you go to a store. You_____ a shirt and buy it.
4. The students are going to _____ a party for the last day of classes.
5. A hippopotamus is _____ than a camel.
6. Robert _____ his leg while he was skiing.
7. The International Student _____ is going to have a dance on Saturday night.

C. Vocabulary Review
Match the words that mean the same.

Column A		Column B	
1.	gift _____	a.	maybe
2.	pleased _____	b.	between
3.	great _____	c.	think
4.	among _____	d.	ruler
5.	leader _____	e.	shave
6.	completely _____	f.	wonderful
7.	fewer _____	g.	sled
8.	pretty _____	h.	present
9.	suppose _____	i.	cows
10.	perhaps _____	j.	less
11.	cattle _____	k.	glad
		l.	all
		m.	beautiful

D. Questions

1. When did the first mountain climbers reach the top of Mount Everest?
2. Where is Mount Everest?
3. Is Mount Everest an ordinary mountain? Why?
4. Who was the first woman to climb Mount Everest?
5. Who organized the climb?
6. What happened to ten of the women climbers?
7. Is Ms. Tabei a big woman?
*8. Is she an ordinary housewife?

9. Where did she practice before she climbed Mount Everest?

10. What did she think when she reached the top?

*11. What is the weather like on Mount Everest?

*12. Is mountain climbing dangerous?

*13. Who paid for the Japanese women's climb?

E. Comprehension

*1. When people climb Mount Everest, most of them start in _____ .
   a. China   c. India
   b. New Zealand   d. Nepal

2. Two people climbed Mount Everest in 1953. They were from _____ .
   a. Japan   c. Nepal
   b. New Zealand   d. b and c

3. _____ Japanese women started to climb Mount Everest.
   a. one   c. two
   b. five   d. fifteen

4. A company in _____ organized the climb.
   a. Tokyo   c. Nepal
   b. Hokkaido   d. New Zealand

5. _____ injured ten of the women.
   a. A club   c. An avalanche
   b. An ordinary   d. A storm

6. Junko Tabei's age was _____ when she climbed the highest mountain in the world.
   a. 25   c. 35
   b. 30   d. 40

*7. Ms. Tabei practiced climbing for _____ years before she climbed Mount Everest.
   a. 15   c. 30
   b. 25   d. 35

8. She was _____ that she was at the top of Mount Everest.
   a. afraid   c. happy
   b. safe   d. a and b

F. Main Idea

1. Junko Tabei, a 35-year-old Japanese, was the first woman to climb Mount Everest.
2. Junko Tabei, a small Japanese woman, practiced climbing mountains for fifteen years.
3. Junko Tabei, an ordinary housewife, was glad when she reached the top of Mount Everest.

THE EUROPEAN RAJA OF SARAWAK

4

James Brooke (1803–1868) was born in India. However, he was British, not Indian. India was a British colony at that time, and James's father was an official in the colonial government.

5   James attended school in England, and then he went into the army. He was injured in a war in Burma, so he left the army. He bought a boat and explored the islands off the coast of Asia.

    Sarawak is on one of these islands. The
10 name of the island is Kalimantan. Today most of Kalimantan **belongs to** Indonesia. While Mr. Brooke was traveling in Asia, there were problems in Sarawak. Some of the people did not like their leader, the **raja**, so they started fighting against
15 him. The fighting continued, and the raja couldn't stop it. Finally, he asked Mr. Brooke for help.

    Mr. Brooke asked the British **navy** to help him. They soon **defeated** the raja's enemies. When the war was <u>over</u>, the raja asked Mr. Brooke   finished
20 to be the ruler of Sarawak. He became the raja. It was very unusual to have a European raja in Asia.

    He was a good ruler. He organized a strong government, and there was no more fighting. Some of the people in the **jungle** were head hunters.   tropical forest

25 They killed people and kept their heads. He made
them stop.

After James Brooke's **death**, his son became   *noun for die*
raja.

Today Sarawak is part of Malaysia. Malaysia
30 is an **independent** country instead of a British
colony. Sarawak has a **governor** but he is not
British. There are no more British rulers in
Sarawak or Malaysia.

A. Vocabulary

belongs to	jungle	colonial	death
Kalimantan	governor	problems	navy
raja	independent	over	defeated

1. Sarawak has a _____ but he is not British.
2. Some of the people did not like their leader, the _____ .
3. Mr. Brooke asked the British _____ to help him.
4. Today most of Kalimantan _____ Indonesia.
5. Malaysia is an _____ country instead of a British colony.
6. They soon _____ the raja's enemies.
7. After James Brooke's _____ , his son became raja.
8. When the war was_____ , the raja asked Mr. Brooke to be the
   ruler of Sarawak.
9. Some of the people in the _____ were head hunters.

B. Vocabulary (new context)

defeated	death	belong to	jungle
governor	navy	against	over
attend	colonial	independent	Sarawak

1. The Tasadays live in the _____ in the Philippines.
2. Every state in the United States has a _____ .
3. Our university _____ the other university in the ball game last night.
4. Gary is in the army. His brother is a sailor in the _____ .
5. The class begins at 11:00. It is _____ at 11:50.
6. Elizabeth II became queen after the _____ of her father.
7. Whom does this jacket _____ ? I found it in our classroom yesterday.
8. All of the old African colonies are _____ countries now.

C. Vocabulary Review
Underline the word that does not belong with the others.

1. double, once, twice, two
2. going to, might, maybe, perhaps
3. giraffe, hippo, camel, locust
4. agree, pleased, glad, happy
5. see, teach, explore, ring
6. yearly, completely, monthly, weekly
7. heavy, thick, gift, ordinary
8. middle, common, ordinary, usual
9. best, worst, oldest, farthest

D. Questions

1. When did James Brooke die?
*2. What century did he live in?
3. Was he Indian?
4. What did he do after he finished school?

5. Why did he leave the army?
6. What did he do after he left the army?
7. Where is Sarawak?
8. What were the problems in Sarawak?
*9. Why did the raja ask Mr. Brooke to become the ruler?
10. Was Mr. Brooke a good ruler?
11. Is Sarawak a colony today?

E. Comprehension: Sequence
Number these sentences in the right order. The first one is done for you.

_____ Mr. Brooke defeated the raja's enemies.
_____ James went to England to study.
_____ Mr. Brooke became the raja of Sarawak.
_____ Sarawak became part of Malaysia.
_____ Mr. Brooke was injured.
_____ Mr. Brooke organized a strong government.
____1___ James Brooke was born in India.
_____ Mr. Brooke died in 1868.
_____ Some of the people fought against the raja.
_____ Mr. Brooke's son became raja.

F. Main Idea

1. James Brooke was English but he was born in India.
2. An Englishman became the raja of an Asian country.
3. James Brooke was a good ruler and he organized a strong government.

A WALK TO
THE NORTH POLE

5

In April 1984, David Hempleman-Adams walked
through **northern** Canada to the North Pole **by
himself.** He walked 400 kilometers in 22 days.

alone

David is an explorer and **adventurer**. He was
the first person to walk to the North Pole by
himself. He was 27 years old when he did it. Other
people traveled to the North Pole before David,
but they had a sled and a dog **team**. David didn't
have a dog team.

10 One day he fell through some thin ice into the
Arctic Ocean. He went into the water above his
knees. He was very **lucky** that he didn't go all the
way into the water. No one could live in that icy water.

At night David slept in a tent. One night a
polar bear tried to pull him out of his tent. He had
15 to **shoot** it. He didn't want to kill the bear, but he
knew the bear wanted to kill him.

The Canadian government says that people
cannot kill polar bears because there are only a few
of them left. Canadian officials sent four people in
20 a plane to talk to David. They saw the bear's
footprints inside the tent. They knew that David
killed the bear to save his own life, so of course they
did not **arrest** him.

David was a **brave** man to go on this adventure
25 by himself. He was also a lucky man because the bear
and the icy water didn't kill him.

EXPLORATION AND ADVENTURE ✦✦✦✦✦

A. Vocabulary

by himself	northern	lucky	brave
adventure	adventurer	footprints	team
icy	arrest	knees	shoot

1. David is an explorer and _____ .
2. He had to _____ it.
3. David was a _____ man to go on this adventure by himself.
4. They saw the bear's _____ .
5. He went into the water above his _____ .
6. In April 1984, David Hempleman-Adams walked through northern Canada to the North Pole _____ .
7. He was very _____ that he didn't go all the way into the water.
8. Other people traveled to the North Pole before David, but they had a sled and a dog _____ .
9. Of course they did not _____ him.

B. Vocabulary (new context)

tent	footprints	brave	by myself
lucky	adventurer	officials	knees
arrest	adventure	shoots	team

1. Our volleyball _____ won the game.
2. I don't need your help. I can do it _____ .
3. Junko Tabei had a great _____ when she climbed Mount Everest.
4. Lois lost her new gold pen but then she found it in her car. She was very

   _____ .
5. When a hunter finds an animal, he usually _____ it.
6. Your _____ are in the middle of your legs.
7. When you walk on the beach, you leave your _____ in the sand.
8. Junko Tabei is a _____ woman.
9. The police will _____ you if you drive 100 kilometers an hour in the city.

C. Vocabulary Review

pickup	competition	map	shells
history	canoe	current	silver
gold	ambassador	jewelry	used to
club	chose	able	future

1. The student _____ someone to answer the next exercise.
2. Carol has some beautiful _____ . Some of it is _____ and some is _____ .
3. Did you have to study the _____ of North America?
4. The new _____ from France met with Queen Elizabeth.
5. Most Europeans can't get _____ Arabic music. It sounds strange to them.
6. Can you find Sarawak, India, and Burma on the _____ ? Are you _____ to find them?
7. Paul belongs to a photography _____ because he likes to take pictures.
8. It is fun to ride on a like in a _____ .
9. A _____ truck is very useful for a carpenter.
10. The Peru _____ brings cold water from Antarctica along the west coast of South America.

D. Questions

1. In what month did David Hempleman-Adams walk to the North Pole?
*2. What was the weather like then?
3. Did David have a dog team?
4. How many people traveled with him?
5. How far did he go into the water?
6. Why did he kill a polar bear?
7. Why did Canadian officials send people to talk to David?
8. How did they know the bear went into the tent?
9. Did they arrest him?
10. Why was David brave?
*11. Was the trip dangerous? Why?
*12. How do you suppose the officials knew about the bear?

E. Comprehension: True/False/No Information

_____ 1. David talked to Canadian officials by radio.

_____ 2. He walked 400 kilometers.

_____ 3. David is a young man.

_____ 4. Other people walked to the North Pole by themselves.

_____ 5. David's dog team carried his tent and food on a sled.

_____ 6. David attended university for four years.

_____ 7. It is cold in northern Canada even in the spring.

_____ 8. David had to kill the bear.

_____ 9. The police went to talk to David.

_____10. They arrested David because he killed the bear.

_____11. David had a radio with him.

F. Main Idea

1. David Hempleman-Adams was the first person to walk to the North Pole alone.
2. David Hempleman-Adams spent twenty-two days walking to the North Pole.
3. A bear almost killed David Hempleman-Adams while he was sleeping.

WORD STUDY

A. Past Continuous

The past continuous is like the present continuous, but it shows something that continued to happen in the past. Use **was/were** instead of **am/is/are** and the **-ing** form of the verb.

Example: It is 5:00. Glen **is studying**.
At 5:00 yesterday, Glen **was studying**.

We often use the past continuous to show that one action interrupted another action. Use the simple past for the other verb.

Example: Glen **was studying** when the phone **rang**.
The phone **rang** while Glen **was studying**.

We usually use the past after **when** and the past continuous after **while**. (**when** + past, **while** + past continuous)

Put the correct form of the verb in the blank.

1. While Mr. Brooke (travel) _____ in Asia, there (be) _____ problems in Sarawak.
2. While David (walk) _____ , he (fall) _____ through the ice.
3. A bear (try) _____ to pull him out of his tent while he (sleep) _____ .
4. Howard (injure) _____ his knee while he (play) _____ soccer.
5. At 7:00 yesterday, David (shave) _____ .
6. Tony (ski) _____ when it (start) _____ to snow.
7. Ann (enter) _____ the building when she (see) _____ an old friend.
8. Jean (sleep) _____ when the doorbell (ring) _____ .

9. Ali (leave) _____ the classroom when the teacher (speak) _____ to him.
10. While Marie (write) _____ a letter, Pierre (telephone) _____ her.

B. Spelling Review

1. **Add y to these nouns. Make an adjective.**

   noise   storm   rock   wave

2. **Add ing to these verbs.**

   study   plan   write   go
   swim   fly   bring   come

3. **Write the plural form of these nouns.**

   century   sandwich   knife   child
   adventure   gift   governor   day

4. **Write the past tense of these verbs.**

   try   mix   drip   belong
   defeat   shop   carry   play

5. **Add est to these adjectives.**

   big   thick   heavy   low
   high   safe   small   hot

C. Word Forms

	Verb	Noun	Adjective
1.		danger	dangerous
2.	invent	invention inventor	
3.		science scientist	scientific
4.	explore	exploration explorer	
5.	sail	sail sailor	
6.	be born	birth	
7.	lead	leader	
8.	rule	ruler	
9.	organize	organization	
10.	injure	injury	

Put the right word form in the blanks. Choose a word from 1 for sentence 1, and so on. Use the right tenses. Some nouns are plural.

1. Always think about the _____ when you walk across the street.
2. The computer is a wonderful _____ .
3. Kumiko plans to study_____ and be a_____ .
4. Captain Cook _____ the Pacific Ocean in the eighteenth century. He was an _____ .
5. _____ did the work on sailing ships. These ships had _____ to catch the wind. The ships_____ all over the world.
6. The _____ of a child makes the family very happy.
7. The captain will _____ the soldiers into the town.
8. A king _____ his country. He might be a good _____ and he might not be.
9. You need to _____ your compositions better. Good _____ is important in compositions.
10. Oscar's car hit a tree. He has several _____ .

EXPLORATION AND ADVENTURE

D. Irregular Verbs

1. Learn these verb forms. Use the past of each one in a sentence.

Simple	Past	Simple	Past
a. choose	chose	e. fall	fell
b. leave	left	f. meet	met
c. spend	spent	g. sleep	slept
d. send	sent	h. understand	understood

2. Write the past tense of these verbs.

a. be
b. blow
c. do
d. get
e. know
f. ring

g. begin
h. cut
i. find
j. give
k. put
l. sell

E. Context Clues

1. Tony and Ann got married three years ago. Then they started fighting a lot. Now they are living **apart**. They live in different apartments.
   a. above
   b. among
   c. not together
   d. agree

2. Ali put a **strip** of paper in his book so he could remember what page he was on.
   a. heavy piece
   b. dark piece
   c. long thin piece
   d. dirty piece

3. There is a **row** of trees along each side of our street.
   a. line
   b. forest
   c. jungle
   d. beard

4. Half a **dozen** eggs is six eggs.
   a. fourteen
   b. twelve
   c. eight
   d. sixteen

5. Paper is **flexible**. Wood and stone are not **flexible**.
    a. You can pick it up.   c. You can move it back and forth.
    b. You can carry it.   d. You can hit it.

6. The paper carrier **delivers** a newspaper to my apartment every morning. I
    don't have to go out and buy one.
    a. hurries   c. defeats
    b. brings   d. buys

7. I tried to pay the government worker for helping me. She didn't **accept** the
    money. The government pays her and she didn't want my money.
    a. bring   c. take
    b. shoot   d. suppose

8. Sam **received** a package from his parents yesterday. It was a birthday present.
    a. brought   c. spent
    b. got   d. told

9. Stop talking **immediately**! The test started five minutes ago.
    a. soon   c. daily
    b. possibly   d. right now

10. Mr. Rubin is a **pilot** for British Airways. He flies airplanes all over the world.
    a. businessman   c. driver of an airplane
    b. carpenter   d. writer for a newspaper

11. There are no classes this afternoon. You have no homework. You can do
    whatever you like.
    a. anything   c. anytime
    b. anywhere   d. anyone

12. Saudi Arabia has a desert **climate**. Canada has a cold **climate** in winter. The
    climate in Indonesia is tropical.
    a. way the weather is all the time   c. hot and dry
    b. changes in the weather every day d. snow and ice

Unit VIII

INVENTIONS AND INVENTORS

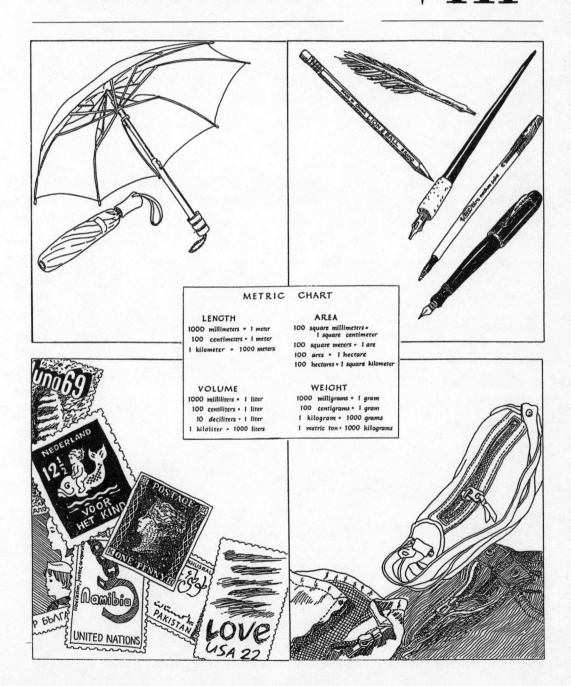

METRIC CHART

LENGTH
1000 millimeters = 1 meter
100 centimeters = 1 meter
1 kilometer = 1000 meters

AREA
100 square millimeters = 1 square centimeter
100 square meters = 1 are
100 ares = 1 hectare
100 hectares = 1 square kilometer

VOLUME
1000 milliliters = 1 liter
100 centiliters = 1 liter
10 deciliters = 1 liter
1 kiloliter = 1000 liters

WEIGHT
1000 milligrams = 1 gram
100 centigrams = 1 gram
1 kilogram = 1000 grams
1 metric ton = 1000 kilograms

THE ZIPPER

1

The **zipper** is a wonderful invention. How did people ever live without zippers? Zippers are very common, so we forget that they are wonderful. They are very strong, but they open and close very
5 easily. They come in many colors and sizes.

In the 1890s, people in the United States wore high shoes with a long **row** of buttons. Women's clothes often had rows of buttons too. People wanted an easier way to put on and take off
10 clothes.

line

Whitcomb L. Judson invented the zipper in 1893. He was an engineer in Chicago. He called the zipper a **slide fastener**. However, it didn't stay closed very well. This was **embarrassing**, and
15 people didn't buy many of them. Then Dr. Gideon Sundback from Sweden solved this problem.

A zipper has three parts. 1. There are **dozens** of metal or plastic **hooks** (called *teeth*) in two rows. 2. These are fastened to two **strips** of cloth.
20 The cloth strips are **flexible**. They **bend** easily. 3. A fastener slides along and fastens the hooks together. When it slides the other way, it takes the hooks **apart**.

a dozen = 12

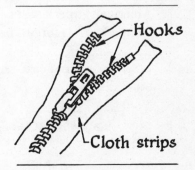

Dr. Sundback put the hooks on the strips of
25 cloth. The cloth holds all the hooks in place. They don't come apart very easily. This solved the problem of the first zippers.

A. Vocabulary

zipper	embarrassing	hooks	dozens
sizes	fastener	flexible	slide
bend	apart	strips	row

1. In the 1890s, people in the United States wore high shoes with a long _____ of buttons.
2. There are _____ of metal or plastic _____ (called *teeth*) in two rows.
3. The _____ is a wonderful invention.
4. The cloth strips are _____ .
5. He called the zipper a_____ _____ .
6. When it slides the other way, it takes the hooks _____ .
7. This was _____ , and people didn't buy many of them.
8. They _____ easily.
9. These are fastened to two _____ of cloth.

B. Vocabulary (new context)

embarrassed	strips	flexible	zippers
hooks	rows	fasteners	bend
apart	dozen	slide	size

1. Icy roads are dangerous because cars _____ on them.
2. Pam cut a piece of paper into _____ .
3. Sometimes your face gets red when you feel _____ .
4. A pencil is not _____ . Paper is.
5. People catch fish with fish <u>_____</u> .
6. Hooks, buttons, and zippers are all _____ .
7. American supermarkets sell eggs by the _____ .
8. Tony and George had an apartment together but now they live _____ .
9. Students sit in a circle in some classes. They sit in _____ in others.
10. You _____ your knees when you sit down.
11. Most pants and jackets have _____ .

C. Vocabulary Review

caves	axe	froze	spirits
map	shells	might	history
canoe	Current	over	death
navy	jungle	independent	shoot

1. Mary's father was in the _____ for twenty years.
2. Did you ever cut wood with an _____ ?
3. What time does the meeting begin, and when will it be_____ ?
4. Carl put water in the freezer part of the refrigerator. It_____ .
5. Giraffes live in grasslands. Some tigers live in the _____ .
6. Carlos had to go back to his country because of a_____ in his family.
7. Some people lived in _____ a long time ago.
8. The Labrador _____ brings cold water from eastern Canada to the east coast of the United States.
9. Students usually have to memorize a lot of dates when they study _____ .
10. Ann and Paula took a long_____ trip on a quiet river during their vacation.
11. Tom is very _____. He likes to think and do things for himself.
12. Soldiers have to learn to _____ guns.

D. Questions

1. Why do we forget that zippers are wonderful?
2. Are zippers strong?
3. What kind of shoes did Americans wear in the 1890s?
4. Who invented the zipper? When did he invent it?
*5. Why is *slide fastener* a good name for a zipper?
6. Why were the first zippers embarrassing?
7. What country was Dr. Sundback from?
8. Describe a zipper. How does it work?
9. What part of the zipper is flexible?
10. What did Dr. Sundback do to make zippers better?
*11. What is a newer kind of fastener than the zipper?

E. Comprehension

1. Zippers open and close by _____ .
   a. shooting
   b. sliding
   c. bending
   d. choosing

2. The hooks are _____ .
   a. plastic
   b. metal
   c. cloth
   d. a and b

3. Mr. Judson was an _____ .
   a. engineer
   b. inventor
   c. American
   d. a, b, and c

4. Mr. Judson didn't sell many zippers because _____ .
   a. it was hard to open and close them
   b. people liked rows of buttons
   c. they came open very easily
   d. they had cloth strips

5. Dr. Sundback was _____ .
   a. a Swede
   b. from Chicago
   c. an American
   d. b and c

6. A zipper has two _____ of cloth.
   a. rows
   b. fasteners
   c. strips
   d. buttons

7. _____ are flexible.
   a. The hooks
   b. The rows of buttons
   c. The fasteners
   d. The strips of cloth

8. Dr. Sundback _____ .
   a. invented the zipper
   b. made the zipper better
   c. invented the button hook
   d. invented the slide fastener

F. Main Idea

1. A zipper has hooks, cloth strips, and a slide fastener.
2. People didn't like the first zippers.
3. Mr. Judson and Dr. Sundback gave us a wonderful invention, the zipper.

THE POSTAGE STAMP

Before the invention of the **postage stamp**, it was difficult to send a letter to another country. The sender paid for the letter to travel in his or her own country. Then the person in the other country
5 paid for that part of the trip. If a letter **crossed**   went across
several countries, the problem was worse.

Rowland Hill, a British teacher, had the idea of a postage stamp with gum on the back. The British post office made the first stamps in 1840.
10 They were the Penny Black and the Twopence Blue. A person bought a stamp and put it on a letter. The post office **delivered** the letter. When   took it to the person
people **received** letters, they didn't have to pay   got
anything. The letters were **prepaid**.   paid for before
15 Postage stamps became popular in Great Britain **immediately**. Other countries started   right away, right now
making their own postage stamps very quickly.

There were still problems with international **mail**. Some countries did not want to **accept**   take
20 letters with stamps from another country. Finally, in 1874 a German organized the Universal Postal System. Each country in the UPS agreed to accept letters with prepaid postage from the other **members**. Today the offices of the UPS are in
25 Switzerland. Almost every country in the world is a member of this organization. It takes care of any international mail problems.

Today post offices in every country sell beautiful stamps. Collecting stamps is one of the most
30 popular hobbies in the world, and every stamp collector knows about the Penny Black and the Twopence Blue.

A. Vocabulary

crossed	received	postage	gum
prepaid	members	international	mail
stamp	delivered	immediately	accept

1. When people _____ letters, they didn't have to pay anything.
2. Before the invention of the _____ _____ , it was difficult to send a letter to another country.
3. The post office _____ the letter.
4. Each country in the UPS agreed to accept letters with prepaid postage from the other _____ .
5. If a letter _____ several countries, the problem was worse.
6. Postage stamps became popular in Great Britain _____ .
7. Some countries did not want to _____ letters with stamps from other countries.
8. The letters were _____ .
9. There were still problems with international _____ .

B. Vocabulary (new context)

prepay	cross	postage	members
deliver	worse	mail	immediately
accept	stamps	international	receive

1. Ali and Marie are _____ of the International Students Club.
2. When you rent an apartment for a year, you have to _____ the last month's rent. You pay the first and the last month's rent.
3. Children have to be careful when they _____ the street.

4. Mr. Ross is going to go to the post office because he has to buy some

   _____ .

5. If you buy living room furniture, the store will _____ it to your house.

6. How much is the _____ for an airmail letter to Japan?

7. Did you _____ any letters this week?

8. Please go to your office _____ . You have a phone call.

9. The teacher will not _____ homework if it is a week late. She won't take it.

10. Did you get any _____ today?

C. Vocabulary Review: Opposites
Match the words that mean the opposite.

Column A	Column B
1. apart _____	a. top
2. bought _____	b. left
3. found _____	c. suppose
4. arrived _____	d. spent
5. bottom _____	e. took
6. be sure _____	f. unable
7. glad _____	g. gold
8. unusual _____	h. choose
9. able _____	i. finally
10. birth _____	j. afraid
11. saved _____	k. together
12. at first _____	l. death
13. brave _____	m. ordinary
14. left _____	n. sold
	o. unhappy
	p. lost

D. Questions

1. Why was it difficult to send a letter to another country before the invention of the postage stamp?
2. Who invented the postage stamp?
3. When did he invent it?
4. What country was he from?
5. Were postage stamps popular?
*6. Why were they popular?
7. What does "prepaid" mean?
*8. Why didn't countries want to accept mail with stamps from other countries?
9. What does the Universal Postal System do today?
10. Where are its offices?
*11. Why do people like to collect stamps?
*12. Why do stamp collectors know about the Penny Black?

E. Comprehension: True/False/No Information

_____ 1. Before postage stamps, two people paid for letters to travel in two countries.
_____ 2. A teacher invented the postage stamp.
_____ 3. He was American.
_____ 4. The first two stamps were colored black and blue.
_____ 5. A stamp shows that the postage is prepaid.
_____ 6. The United States was the second country to make postage stamps.
_____ 7. Postage stamps solved all mail problems immediately.
_____ 8. Members of the UPS accept prepaid letters from other countries.
_____ 9. Kuwait is a member of the UPS.
_____ 10. All the UPS officials are Swiss.
_____ 11. Stamp collecting is a popular hobby.

F. Main Idea

1. Rowland Hill, a British teacher, invented the postage stamp.
2. When Mr. Hill invented the postage stamp, it solved a lot of mail problems.
3. People collect stamps because every country makes beautiful ones.

PENCILS AND PENS

3

No one knows who invented pencils or when it happened. A Swiss described a pencil in a book in 1565. He said it was a piece of wood with **lead** (Pb) inside it. (Lead is a very soft, heavy metal.) Pencils
5 weren't popular, and people continued to write with pens. They used bird feathers as pens.

Then in 1795 someone started making pencils from **graphite**, and they became very popular. Graphite is a kind of **coal**. (Coal is black and we
10 burn it for heat and energy.) Today people make pencils in the same way. They **grind** the graphite, make it into the shape of a stick, and bake it. Then they put it inside a piece of wood. One pencil can write 50,000 English words or make a line 55
15 kilometers long.

People wrote with feather pens and then used pens with metal **points**. They had to **dip** the point into **ink** after every few letters. Next someone invented a **fountain pen** that could hold ink inside
20 it. A fountain pen can write several pages before you have to fill it again.

Two Hungarian brothers, Ladislao and Georg Biro, invented the **ballpoint** pen that we all use today. They left Hungary and started
25 making ballpoint pens in England in 1943 during the Second World War. English **pilots** liked them.

drivers of airplanes

They couldn't write with fountain pens in airplanes because the ink **leaked** out. Later, a French company called Bic bought the Biro's company.

30   Some people call ballpoint pens a bic. Australians call them biros. **Whatever** we call them, we use them every day.

anything

A. Vocabulary

ballpoint	points	graphite	lead
coal	dip	whatever	leaked
grind	pilots	ink	fountain pen

1. English _____ couldn't write with fountain pens in airplanes because the ink _____ out.
2. Then in 1795 someone started making pencils from _____, and they became very popular.
3. He said it was a piece of wood with _____ (Pb) inside it.
4. People wrote with feather pens and then used pens with metal _____ .
5. Graphite is a kind of _____ .
6. Next someone invented a _____ that could hold ink inside it.
7. They had to _____ the point into _____ after every few letters.
8. They _____ the graphite, make it into the shape of a stick, and bake it.
9. Two Hungarian brothers, Ladislao and Georg Biro, invented the _____ pen that we all use today.
10. _____ we call them, we use them every day.

B. Vocabulary (new context)

graphite	ballpoint	pilot	lead
coal	leaks	grind	fountain pen
ink	point	dips	whatever

INVENTIONS AND INVENTORS

1. Our shower _____ . A little water runs out of it all day.
2. Dead plants and animals became _____ and petroleum millions of years ago.
3. You should have a good _____ on your pencil.
4. Yoko's brother is a _____ . He flies for Japan Airlines.
5. _____ is a soft, heavy metal.
6. Students a hundred years ago always had a bottle of_____ on their desks.
7. Dan works in an ice cream store. He _____ the ice cream into dishes and onto cones.
8. We _____ coffee before we mix it with hot water.
9. Most people use _____ pens, but some people like a _____ _____ .
10. At a cafeteria, you can choose _____ you want to eat.

C. Vocabulary Review

by herself	team	lucky	arrested
size	apart	slide	embarrassed
strip	bend	row	fastener
dozen	hook	flexible	axe

1. There are about a _____ students in the class. It is a small class.
2. Mountain climbers always carry a little _____ with them.
3. What _____ cola do you want, small or large?
4. People often _____ over when they talk to children.
5. A children's park always has a slide. Children can_____ down it.
6. My little daughter is pleased that she can get dressed _____ now.
7. Masako was_____ when she gave the wrong answer in class.
8. How many people are on a soccer _____ ?
9. Robert took his bicycle _____ and now he can't put it back together again.
10. There is a_____ on the back of the door. You can hang your jacket there.
11. The police _____ the boy who took my bicycle.
12. Maria always sits in the front _____ of the class.

D. Questions

1. Who invented the pencil? When?
2. Describe the pencils of 1565.
3. Describe a modern pencil.
4. How do people make pencils today?
5. What kind of pens did people write with after feather pens?
6. Why was a fountain pen better than the old pens?
7. Where were the inventors of the ballpoint pen from?
8. Why is a ballpoint better than a fountain pen for pilots?
*9. Why does a fountain pen leak in an airplane?
10. In what country are Bic pens made?
*11. Where did the name *biro* come from?
*12. Which is better, a pencil or a ballpoint pen?

E. Comprehension

1. _____ described a pencil in 1565.
   a. A Hungarian
   b. A Swiss
   c. A Frenchman
   d. An Englishman

2. The first pencils had _____ in them.
   a. gold
   b. graphite
   c. lead
   d. ink

3. One pencil can write _____ words.
   a. 50,000
   b. 55,000
   c. 55
   d. 1565

4. The first pens were _____ .
   a. wooden
   b. feathers
   c. metal
   d. graphite

5. The next pens had a _____ point.
   a. wooden
   b. lead
   c. metal
   d. silver

6. A fountain pen can hold _____ inside it.
   a. coal
   b. lead
   c. graphite
   d. ink

7. The Biro brothers made thousands of pens in _____ .
   a. England
   b. Hungary
   c. France
   d. Switzerland

*8. _____ are best for writing in airplanes.
   a. Ballpoint pens
   b. Pencils
   c. Fountain pens
   d. a and b

*9. People burn _____ .
   a. coal and graphite
   b. graphite and lead
   c. coal and wood
   d. lead and coal

*10. People grind _____ .
   a. hamburger meat
   b. coffee
   c. graphite
   d. a, b, and c

F. Main Idea

1. There were several kinds of pens before ballpoint pens.
2. We use pens and pencils every day.
3. Ballpoint pens and pencils are very useful inventions.

UMBRELLAS

4

The umbrella is a very ordinary **object**. It keeps the rain and the sun off people. Some umbrellas **fold up**, so it is easy to carry them.

thing

However, the umbrella did not begin life as an
5 ordinary object. It was a sign of **royalty** or importance. Some African **tribes** still use umbrellas in this way today. Someone carries an umbrella and walks behind the king or important person.

kings, queens, and their families

Umbrellas are very old. The Chinese had
15 them in the eleventh century B.C. From China they traveled to India, Persia, and Egypt. In Greece and Rome, men **wouldn't** use them. They believed umbrellas were only for women.

past of won't

When the Spanish explorers went to Mexico,
15 they saw the Aztec kings using umbrellas. English explorers saw Indian **princes** carrying umbrellas on the east coast of North America. It **seems** that people in different parts of the world invented umbrellas at different times.

sons of queens and kings

20 England was probably the first country in Europe where ordinary people used umbrellas against the rain. England has a rainy **climate**, and umbrellas are very useful there.

Everybody uses umbrellas today. The next
25 time you carry one, remember that for centuries only great men and women used them. Perhaps you are really a king or queen, a **princess** or prince.

daughter of a king and queen

A. Vocabulary

wouldn't	queens	princes	princess
king	object	climate	tribes
royalty	importance	fold up	seems

1. English explorers saw Indian _____ carrying umbrellas on the east coast of North America.
2. It was a sign of _____ or importance.
3. England has a rainy _____ , and umbrellas are very useful there.
4. The umbrella is a very ordinary _____ .
5. In Greece and Rome, men _____ use them.
6. Perhaps you are really a king or queen, a _____ or prince.
7. Some African _____ still use umbrellas in this way today.
8. Some umbrellas _____ , so it is easy to carry them.
9. It _____ that people in different parts of the world invented umbrellas at different times.

B. Vocabulary (new context)

prince	princess	objects	seems
importance	fold	wouldn't	climate
queen	king	royalty	tribe

1. A _____ is the daughter of a king or queen. A _____ is the son of a king and queen. They are all _____ .
2. Bill _____ very unhappy today. What is wrong?
3. The Tasadays had no metal. They only had _____ made of wood and stone.
4. Dan asked Maria to go to the movies with him last night, but she _____ go. She was too tired.
5. The Hopis are an Indian _____ in Arizona.
6. Qatar has a desert _____ , but Malaysia is in the tropics.
7. After you write a letter, you _____ it and put it in an envelope.

C. Vocabulary Review
Underline the word that does not belong.

1. around, about, nearly, behind
2. movie theater, art museum, gymnasium, science museum
3. governor, collector, traveler, sailor
4. jungle, navy, forest, trees
5. game, team, win, adventure
6. dozen, eighteen, kilo, eleven
7. hook, button, flexible, zipper
8. slide, receive, take, accept
9. lead, gold, coal, silver
10. put, run, cut, hit

D. Questions

1. What are two uses of an umbrella?
*2. Why is it easier to carry an umbrella that folds up?
3. What was an umbrella a sign of in the past?
4. Who uses umbrellas in this way today?
*5. How do we know that the Chinese had umbrellas in the eleventh century B.C.?
6. Why didn't Greek men use umbrellas?
7. What other people invented the umbrella?
8. Why did English people like umbrellas?
*9. In what countries are umbrellas not very useful?

E. Comprehension

1. Today people use umbrellas for _____ .
   a. the rain
   b. the sun
   c. a sign of a great person
   d. a, b, and c

2. A queen is a _____ person.
   a. royal
   b. embarrassing
   c. holiday
   d. jewelry

3. A great person walks _____ someone with an umbrella.
   a. beside
   b. before
   c. in front of
   d. in back of

4. India and Persia learned about umbrellas from _____ .
   a. Aztec Indians
   b. Egypt
   c. China
   d. Spanish explorers

*5. Most groups of people had some kind of _____ .
   a. coal
   b. royalty
   c. ink
   d. mail

6. American Indians _____ .
   a. learned about umbrellas from English and Spanish explorers
   b. invented umbrellas
   c. got umbrellas from the Chinese
   d. taught Egyptians about umbrellas

7. English people started using umbrellas because they have _____ .
   a. royalty
   b. a rainy climate
   c. too much sun
   d. great men and women

F. Main Idea

1. For centuries only great people used umbrellas, but now ordinary people everywhere use them.
2. Umbrellas are useful in the rain.
3. The Chinese and American Indians invented umbrellas.

THE METRIC SYSTEM

5

People all over the world use kilograms, centimeters, square meters, liters, and Celsius (C). These are all ways to **measure** things. They are all part of the **metric system**.

During the French **Revolution** (1789–1799) against the king, the revolutionary government started the metric system. Before that, every part of France had a different system for measuring things. Also, cloth makers measured cloth with one system. Jewelers used another system. Carpenters used another. Other countries used other systems. The revolutionary government wanted one international scientific system of measurement. They asked a group of scientists and mathematicians to invent a system.

The mathematicians and scientists **decided** to use the numbers ten, hundred, and thousand for their system.

Next they had to decide on a "natural" **length**. They chose one ten-millionth (1/10,000,000) of the **distance** from the **Equator** to the North Pole. They called this one meter. Then they chose one gram for weighing things. A **cubic** centimeter of water weighs one gram.

Mathematicians and scientists worked on these problems for twenty years until they finally

war by the people against their government

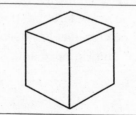

noun for *long*

distance = how far

finished the complete system. The biggest problem was measuring the meter.

The metric system was a wonderful gift to the
30 world. There are only five countries that don't use
it. They are Brunei, Burma, North and South
Yemen, and the United States. The metric system
is truly an international system.

A. Vocabulary

Revolution	decided	cubic	measure
centimeters	Equator	metric	length
ten-millionth	system	Celsius	distance

1. During the French _____ (1789–1799) against the king, the
   revolutionary government started the metric system.
2. Next they had to decide on a "natural" _____ .
3. They are all part of the _____ _____ .
4. A _____ centimeter of water weighs one gram.
5. They chose one ten-millionth of the _____ from the
   _____ to the North Pole.
6. These are all ways to _____ things.
7. The mathematicians and scientists _____ to use the numbers
   ten, hundred, and thousand for their system.

B. Vocabulary (new context)

liter	Revolution	Equator	cube
square	system	length	metric
distance	measure	decided	gram

1. The Russian _____ in 1917 was against the royal family of Russia.
2. What is the _____ between Chicago and New York?
3. The _____ system is a system of measurement.
4. Junko Tabei, a Japanese housewife, _____ to try to climb Mount Everest.
5. We need to buy a tablecloth. Please _____ the table so we will know what size to buy. What is the _____ of the table? How long is it?
6. Indonesia, Kenya, and the Amazon area are all on the _____ .
7. A _____ has six sides. Each side is the same size.
8. The British had the first _____ of prepaid postage.

C. Vocabulary Review

lonely	evaporated	percent	basket
broom	section	tires	crossed
postage	deliver	prepaid	stamp
immediately	member	point	chew

1. Keiko doesn't like to be away from her family. She feels _____ .
2. Lamb and beef are in the meat _____ of a supermarket.
3. Ninety-five _____ of the class passed the test.
4. Letters that go outside a country take more _____ than letters inside a country.
5. Alice came in from the garden with a _____ of beautiful flowers.
6. Did the mail carrier _____ the mail yet?
7. The _____ on my pencil is broken. May I sharpen it?
8. Some people do not like to _____ gum.
9. There is no water left in the dish. It all _____ .

10. We need two new front _____ for the car.
11. The Polynesians _____ the Pacific Ocean in double canoes.
12. Carl is a _____ of the stamp club. Collecting stamps is his hobby.

D. Questions

*1. What do **centi-** and **milli-** mean?
2. What is the metric system?
3. Who was the French Revolution against?
4. Before the Revolution, there was a problem in France about measuring things. What was it?
5. Who invented the metric system?
6. What did they choose for the "natural" length?
7. How did they choose one gram?
8. How long did it take to complete the system?
9. Why do we call this an international system of measurement?
*10. Why is the metric system easy to use?

E. Comprehension: True/False/No Information

_____ 1. Celsius is part of the metric system.
_____ 2. Hectares are part of the metric system.
_____ 3. We use the metric system to measure things.
_____ 4. The French Revolution was in the seventeenth century.
_____ 5. The metric system is an international scientific system of measurement.
_____ 6. A mathematician and a scientist invented the metric system.
_____ 7. France gave the world a wonderful gift.
_____ 8. The United States uses the metric system.
_____ 9. The United States uses an old English system of measurement.
_____ 10. The French Revolution was after the American Revolution.

F. Main Idea

Put the letter of the details after the main ideas. Some details go with more than one main idea.

1. **The Zipper**

2. **The Postage Stamp**

3. **The Pencil**

4. **The Ballpoint Pen**

5. **The Umbrella**

6. **The Metric System**

    a. A British teacher invented it.
    b. French scientists and mathematicians invented it.
    c. Different groups of people invented it.
    d. An American invented it.
    e. No one knows who invented it.
    f. Two Hungarian brothers invented it.
    g. It is international and scientific.
    h. Sometimes it is a sign of royalty.
    i. The United States doesn't use it.
    j. It is a fastener.
    k. One of them can write 50,000 words.
    l. It is better than a fountain pen in an airplane.
    m. People in many countries use it.
    n. Collecting them is a popular hobby.

INVENTIONS AND INVENTORS

WORD STUDY

A. Will/Be going to
There are two ways to write about the future in English.

1. **Will + simple verb**

   Example: Carol **will lend** me her car tomorrow.
   Classes **will end** next week.

2. **Be (am, is, are) + going to + simple verb**

   Example: The store **is going to deliver** our new refrigerator this afternoon.
   I **am going to measure** the kitchen floor.

   1. Write sentences with **will** and the word in parentheses.

      Example: travel (next summer)
      My parents **will travel** in Japan for two months next summer.

      a. receive   (next week)
      b. deliver   (tomorrow)
      c. decide   (tonight)
      d. arrive   (tomorrow morning)
      e. go skiing   (next winter)

   2. Write sentences with **be going to** and the words in parentheses.

      Example: attend (next week)
      I **am going to attend** my cousin's wedding next week.

      a. continue   (next fall)
      b. practice   (all summer)
      c. choose   (tomorrow)
      d. roast   (tonight)
      e. leave   (next month)

B. How + Adjective

Examples: **How far** is it to Los Angeles?
How old are you?
How large is your country?
How heavy is a hippopotamus?

Use these words in questions.

1. how long
2. how deep
3. how tall
4. how much
5. how fast

C. Irregular Verbs

1. Learn these verb forms. Then use each past form in a sentence.

Simple	Past	Simple	Past
a. keep	kept	f. freeze	froze
b. hurt	hurt	g. lose	lost
c. lead	led	h. pay	paid
d. write	wrote	i. speak	spoke
e. wear	wore	j. build	built

2. Write the past of these verbs.

a. blow
b. give
c. know
d. drip
e. meet
f. understand

g. choose
h. grow
i. leave
j. hit
k. fall
l. send

INVENTIONS AND INVENTORS

D. Word Forms

	Verb	Noun	Adjective
1.	collect	collection	
		collector	
2.	describe	description	
3.	heat	heat	hot
4.		royalty	royal
5.		importance	important
6.	soften	softener	soft
7.	believe	belief	
8.	rain	rain	rainy
9.	sharpen	sharpener	sharp
10.	measure	measurement	

Put the right word form in the blanks. Use a word from line 1 for sentence 1 and so on. Use the right form of the verb and singular and plural nouns.

1. Lois is a stamp _____ . She _____ stamps. She has a large _____ .
2. Write a _____ of your city. _____ it.
3. We need some _____ water. Please _____ some.
4. Prince Charles is a member of the British _____ family. His parents are _____ too.
5. In India umbrellas were a sign of _____ . Only _____ people used them.
6. Gum has a _____ in it. This _____ the gum so people can chew it. It makes the gum _____ .
7. Many people _____ that God made the earth. This is their _____ .
8. It is starting to _____ . We are going to have a _____ day. Do you like the _____ ?
9. Where is the pencil _____ ? My pencil isn't _____ . I need to _____ it.
10. Please _____ the size of the living room carpet. How long and how wide is it? What are the _____ ?

E. Context Clues

1. It is very cold in Norway in winter. You have to wear a heavy coat, a hat on your head, and **gloves** on your hands.
   a. something to keep the hands warm
   b. something to make the hands look pretty
   c. something to cool the hands
   d. something that makes the hands work better

2. People cannot ride their bicycles on the **sidewalk** because it is dangerous for the people walking there. They have to ride in the street.
   a. the middle of the street
   b. a place at the side of the street for people to walk
   c. a beautiful part of a park
   d. a place for cars and motorcycles

3. Mr. da Silva's little boy was going to run into the street. Mr. da Silva **yelled** at him to come back.
   a. pushed quickly
   b. arrested
   c. seemed
   d. spoke loudly

4. A hundred years ago people crossed the ocean by ship. This was slow. Today we travel by plane at a **high speed**.
   a. slowly
   b. independently
   c. very fast
   d. luckily

5. Captain Lee **trains** new police officers. The new officers study and practice for their new jobs.
   a. belongs to
   b. teaches
   c. agrees
   d. shaves

6. In a basketball game, one player **passes** the ball to another player.
   a. sends
   b. decides
   c. takes
   d. throws

7. Oman is one of the Arab **nations**.
   a. countries
   b. religions
   c. mountains
   d. governors

8. Barbara had her coffee cup in front of her. When she finished drinking her coffee, she pushed the cup **aside**.
   a. off the table
   b. to the side
   c. into the kitchen
   d. into the air

9. Carol visited all the capital cities in Europe **except** Rome. She didn't have time to go there.
   a. when
   b. so
   c. but
   d. that

10. I'm sorry we can't talk any longer, but we are going to be late. We have to **rush**.
    a. hurry
    b. lead
    c. carry
    d. grow

11. Switzerland has beautiful high mountains. However, people can't live high in the mountains because life there is too difficult. They live in the **valleys**.
    a. large cities on grasslands
    b. tropical forests
    c. low areas between mountains
    d. hot desert areas

12. Today is my younger brother's sports day. There are games all morning. In the afternoon he is going to run in a foot **race**.
    a. volleyball game
    b. running competition
    c. competition among horses
    d. skiing competition

13. Running is usually an **individual** sport. Volleyball and basketball are team sports.
    a. group of people
    b. team
    c. several people together
    d. one person

14. Pierre wrote an **excellent** composition. It is the best one in the class.
    a. very, very good
    b. not interesting
    c. poor
    d. boring

15. The teacher walked **ahead** of the students. He was leading the way to the new classroom.
    a. in back of
    b. near
    c. beside
    d. in front of

16. Coke and Pepsi are **similar** drinks. Seven-Up tastes different.
    a. different
    b. almost the same
    c. fried
    d. dark

Unit

IX

UNUSUAL SPORTS

THAI BOXING

1

Boxing is popular in many countries. Two fighters wear boxing **gloves** on their hands. A bell rings. The boxers hit each other until one **knocks out** the other. Each part of the fight is 3 minutes
5 long. It is called a **round**.

Thai boxing is different. The boxing **match** begins with music from **drums** and **flutes**. Then the two fighters **kneel** and **pray** to God. Next they do a slow dance that copies the movements of Thai
10 boxing. During this dance, each fighter tries to show the other that he is best.

Then the fight begins. In Thai boxing, the fighters can **kick** with their feet and hit each other with their **elbows** and knees. Of course they hit
15 with their hands too. Each round is 3 minutes long. Then the boxers have a 2-minute rest. Most box-ers can fight only five rounds because this kind of fighting is very difficult.

Thai boxing began over 500 years ago. If a
20 soldier lost his **weapons** in a **battle**, he needed to fight with just his body. The soldiers learned how to use all the parts of their body. In 1560, the Burmese army **captured** Naresuen, the King of Thailand, in a war. King Naresuen was a very good
25 boxer. He won his **freedom** from Burma by defeat-ing all the best Burmese fighters. When he re-turned to Thailand, his people were very **proud** of him. Thai boxing became a popular sport.

competition

bend down on the knees

hit with the feet
the part of the arm that bends

battle = a fight

A. Vocabulary

gloves   match   kick   proud
round   weapons   captured   knocks out
kneel   elbows   battle   freedom
copies   pray   flutes   drums

1. The boxers hit each other until one _____ the other.
2. The boxing _____ begins with music from _____ and _____ .
3. In Thai boxing, the fighters can _____ with their feet and hit each other with their _____ and knees.
4. Two fighters wear boxing _____ on their hands.
5. If a soldier lost his _____ in a _____ , he needed to fight with just his body.
6. He won his _____ from Burma by defeating all the best Burmese fighters.
7. It is called a _____ .
8. Then the two fighters _____ and _____ to God.
9. In 1560, the Burmese army _____ Naresuen, the King of Thailand, in a war.
10. When he returned to Thailand, his people were very _____ of him.

B. Vocabulary (new context)

match   copies   kneel   weapons
freedom   drums   flutes   knock
captured   pray   elbows   boxers
gloves   kick   battles   proud

1. It is cold today. You should wear _____ and a hat.
2. Many people of the world make music with _____ and _____ .
3. There is a tennis _____ on television tomorrow afternoon.
4. You have to _____ down when you pick up something on the floor.

5. The scientists _____ a dolphin so they could study it.
6. Your knees are part of your legs. Your _____ are part of your arms.
7. Religious people _____ every day.
8. Nadia got a good grade on her quiz. She is _____ of herself.
9. In soccer you can _____ the ball. In basketball you can throw it.
10. Most countries in the world spend too much money on _____ for the army.
11. There are terrible _____ in a war.
12. Kenya was a British colony. It won its _____ in 1953.

C. Vocabulary Review
Match the words that mean the same.

Column A
1. raw _____
2. caffeine _____
3. object _____
4. distance _____
5. revolution _____
6. Equator _____
7. whatever _____
8. princess _____
9. independent _____
10. over _____
11. roll _____
12. prince _____
13. climate _____

Column B
a. a kind of bread
b. anything
c. the sister of a prince
d. the brother of a princess
e. not cooked
f. war
g. finished
h. free
i. something in coffee and tea
j. weather
k. dip
l. thing
m. how far
n. leak
o. line around the middle of the earth

D. Questions

1. What do boxers wear on their hands?
2. What is one part of a fight called?
3. How does a Thai boxing match begin?

4. What do the boxers do before they start fighting?
5. Why do they do a slow dance?
6. How is Thai boxing different from other boxing?
7. What is the length of a round in Thai boxing?
8. Why did Thai soldiers learn to box?
9. How did King Naresuen win his freedom?
10. How did his people feel about this?
*11. Is boxing safe or dangerous? Why?
*12. Is Thai boxing safer or more dangerous than other boxing? Why?

E. Comprehension

1. Most boxing begins with a _____ .
   a. bell
   b. drum
   c. flute
   d. b and c

2. Thai boxers don't hit with their _____ .
   a. hands
   b. elbows
   c. knees
   d. heads

3. Thai boxers _____ before the fight.
   a. grind
   b. knock out
   c. pray
   d. capture

4. They pray on their _____ .
   a. elbows
   b. backs
   c. hands
   d. knees

5. Thai boxing began _____ .
   a. as a sport
   b. in the navy
   c. in the army
   d. as a dance

6. _____ made Thai boxing a popular sport.
   a. A Burmese
   b. A king
   c. A soldier
   d. The army

7. The king's people were _____ .
   a. proud of him
   b. royalty
   c. defeated
   d. captured

F. Main Idea

1. Thai boxing has music before the match.
2. Most Thai boxers can fight only a short time.
3. Thai boxing is different from other boxing.

CURLING

2

Curling is a popular sport in Canada. However, it probably started in Scotland or Holland around three hundred years ago.

There are two teams with four people on each
5 team in curling. The teams play on a sheet of ice that is 45 meters long and 4.3 meters wide.

Each player slides two heavy stones toward the "house" circle at the opposite end of the ice sheet. The stones weigh almost twenty kilos. Each
10 stone is **flat** on the top and bottom and has a **handle** on the top. The player uses the handle to slide the stone. The player **swings** the stone off the ice and it curls or **curves** as it slides along. It does not go in a **straight** line.

15 While one player throws the stone, his teammates **sweep** in front of the stone This **smooths** the ice. The players believe that the stone travels faster on smooth ice, and it can go farther. The **captain** of the team **yells** "Sweep!" and the
20 teammates start sweeping the ice.

Usually people sweep the floor or the **sidewalk** with a broom. They don't sweep as a sport. Curling is an unusual game.

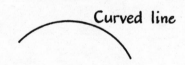

Straight line

Curved line

captain = leader / yells = says loudly

UNUSUAL SPORTS

A. Vocabulary

sweep	teammates	handle	curling
yells	smooths	flat	sidewalk
straight	swings	captain	curves

1. _____ is a popular sport in Canada.
2. The player _____ the stone off the ice, and it curls or _____ as it slides along.
3. Usually people sweep the floor or the _____ .
4. Each stone is _____ on the top and bottom and has a _____ on the top.
5. His teammates _____ in front of the stone.
6. It does not go in a _____ line.
7. The captain of the team _____ "Sweep!" and the teammates start sweeping the ice.
8. This _____ the ice.

B. Vocabulary (new context)

curly	straight	sweep	yelled
sidewalk	teammates	captain	flat
handle	smooth	swing	curves

1. When Gary saw his friend down the street, he _____ to him.
2. Pam's hair is wavy, Ruth's hair is _____ , and Keiko's hair is _____ .
3. Silk is a _____ kind of cloth.
4. Mrs. White is going to cut the grass and _____ the _____ in front of her house.
5. Children like to _____ in the swings at our park.
6. A suitcase has a _____ on it. This makes it easy to carry.
7. You must drive carefully when there are a lot of _____ in the road.
8. Every ship has a _____ .
9. The top of a desk or table is _____ .

C. Vocabulary Review

already	pepper	nuts	either
footprints	pilot	seems	would
folded	tribe	system	decide
cubes	metric	kicked	gloves

1. Please pass me the salt and _____ .
2. What is the temperature? It _____ cold today.
3. You can write with _____ a ballpoint pen or a pencil.
4. There were wet _____ on the floor near the shower.
5. The dancers _____ their feet into the air.
6. The boys were eating popcorn and_____ and drinking cans of Coke while they watched television.
7. Each Arab _____ has its own name.
8. Glen _____ his clothes after he took them out of the dryer.
9. Bob can't _____ what to cook for dinner. He doesn't know what to cook.
10. _____ you like to go out to dinner tonight?
11. Some people buy sugar _____ for their coffee.
12. The _____ _____ uses meters and grams.

D. Questions

1. Where is curling popular?
2. Did Canadians invent this game?
*3. How many people play curling at one time?
*4. Do Canadians play this game in summer?
5. How do the players slide the stones?
*6. Why is this game called curling?
7. Why do the players sweep the ice?
8. When does the captain of the team yell "Sweep!"?

E. Comprehension: True/False

_____ *1. Either the Scots or Dutch invented curling.
_____ *2. Canadians play curling all year round.
_____ 3. They play curling on a sheet of ice.
_____ 4. They play it with a ball.
_____ 5. The players throw small stones.
_____ *6. There are several sports where players slide stones on the ice.
_____ 7. Sweeping the ice makes it smooth.
_____ *8. The stones slide faster on smooth ice.
_____ 9. Team members sweep the ice to clean it.

F. Main Idea

1. Canadians invented and play the unusual game of curling.
2. Curling players sweep and slide stones on the ice.
3. Curling is an unusual game that Canadians play.

LACROSSE

3

Lacrosse is another popular sport in Canada. It is one of the oldest organized sports in America. The Indians in northern New York State and southern Ontario, Canada, invented it. They used
5 it to **train** for war. They invented this game before Columbus arrived in the New World.

practice

People play lacrosse outdoors. The lacrosse **field** is seventy meters long. At each end of the field there is a **goal**. The goal is a **net**. There are
10 ten players on each team. Each player has a stick called a "crosse." The players hit a ball that is 21 centimeters around and weighs 140 grams. They try to hit the ball into the net as many times as possible. Lacrosse is a very fast game because the
15 players can catch and **pass** the ball at a **high speed** with their sticks.

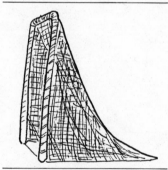

very fast

At one time lacrosse was the **national** summer sport in Canada. It is also popular in Britain and Australia.

UNUSUAL SPORTS

A. Vocabulary

arrived	national	train	high speed
oldest	seventy	goal	lacrosse
net	stick	field	pass

1. At one time lacrosse was the _____ summer sport in Canada.
2. At each end of the field there is a _____ .
3. _____ is another popular sport in Canada.
4. Lacrosse is a very fast game because the players can catch and _____ the ball at a _____ with their sticks.
5. They used it to _____ for war.
6. The lacrosse _____ is seventy meters long.
7. The goal is a _____ .

B. Vocabulary (new context)

training	goal	national	speed
passed	field	net	passed

1. The basketball player _____ the ball to his teammate. The teammate made a basket.
2. New fire fighters get _____ in how to fight fires.
3. In volleyball, the teams hit the ball back and forth across the _____ .
4. What is the _____ of light? How fast does light travel?
5. Each country has a _____ flag. The British, French, and American flags are red, white, and blue.
6. A soccer _____ has a _____ at each end.

C. Vocabulary Review
Match the words that mean the same.

Column A

1. over _____
2. battle _____
3. dozen _____
4. wherever _____
5. match _____
6. object _____
7. accept _____
8. freedom _____
9. row _____
10. receive _____
11. pre- _____
12. adult _____

Column B

a. competition
b. independence
c. thing
d. before
e. take
f. flute
g. fighting
h. pray
i. finished
j. anywhere
k. line
l. twelve
m. get
n. grownup

D. Questions

1. Who invented lacrosse?
*2. How is lacrosse like Thai boxing?
3. What countries play lacrosse?
4. How many goals are there?
5. How many players are on each team?
6. What does each player have?
7. What do the players try to do?
8. Why is lacrosse a fast game?
*9. Why don't they play lacrosse in winter in Canada?
*10. What is an organized sport?

E. Comprehension

1. Lacrosse was the national summer sport in _____ .
   a. Canada
   b. England
   c. Australia
   d. New York State

2. _____ invented lacrosse.
   a. Columbus
   b. Indians
   c. Canadians
   d. A team

3. The Indians invented lacrosse to _____ for war.
   a. fight
   b. pass
   c. train
   d. hang

4. People play lacrosse _____ .
   a. on a field
   b. in a stadium
   c. on a sheet of ice
   d. indoors

*5. _____ people play in a lacrosse game.
   a. Eight
   b. Twenty
   c. Fifteen
   d. Thirty

6. The players _____ .
   a. hit a ball with a stick
   b. hit each other
   c. swing and then slide a stone
   d. kick a ball

7. The players catch and pass the ball very _____ .
   a. quickly
   b. heavily
   c. slowly
   d. yearly

*8. _____ is the national sport of the United States.
   a. Soccer
   b. Boxing
   c. Basketball
   d. Baseball

F. Main Idea

1. The Indians invented lacrosse, a fast game that is popular in Canada.
2. Lacrosse is an outdoor game that is very fast.
3. In lacrosse, two teams use sticks to hit a ball.

SUMO

4

Sumo wrestling is a national sport in Japan. Every year there are six **tournaments**, and millions of Japanese watch them on television. A tournament is a **series** of matches.

one after another

5   Sumo is almost as old as the nation of Japan itself. Stories say that there was sumo wrestling over 2,000 years ago. History says that there were national sumo tournaments in the eighth century.

Usually **athletes** are thin and can move very quickly. It is beautiful to watch them play. However, sumo wrestlers weigh from 100 to 160 kilos. One famous wrestler weighed 195 kilos. Sumo wrestlers do not look beautiful, and sumo wrestling is a very slow sport.

people who play sports well

15   Sumo wrestlers start training when they are boys. They **exercise** to make their bodies strong. They also eat and eat and eat.

Sumo wrestlers wrestle in a round **ring** with a sand floor. A wrestler loses the match if he leaves the ring. He is also the loser if any part of his body **except** his feet **touches** the floor. Each wrestler tries to push the other down on the floor or out of the ring. Sometimes one wrestler just **steps aside** when the other wrestler **rushes** toward him. Then that wrestler falls down or falls out of the ring.

but

aside = to the side
hurries

People from other countries usually think sumo is very strange, but the Japanese love it. Even young people find this traditional sport **exciting**.

exciting ≠ boring

UNUSUAL SPORTS

A. Vocabulary

series	sumo wrestling	ring	except
steps	exercise	athletes	exciting
touches	aside	rushes	tournaments

1. Sometimes one wrestler just _____ _____ when the other wrestler _____ toward him.
2. A tournament is a _____ of matches.
3. He is also the loser if any part of his body _____ his feet _____ the floor.
4. _____ is a national sport in Japan.
5. Even young people find this traditional sport _____ .
6. Usually _____ are thin and can move very quickly.
7. Every year there are six _____ , and millions of Japanese watch them on television.
8. Sumo wrestlers wrestle in a round _____ with a sand floor.
9. They _____ to make their bodies strong.

B. Vocabulary (new context)

athletes	wrestle	rushed	exciting
stepped	tournament	except	exercise
series	touch	aside	ring

1. Sumo is in a round _____ . Thai boxing is in a square one.
2. Only two people box or _____ at the same time.
3. Stan put his math homework _____ . He said he would do it later.
4. _____ play basketball, lacrosse, volleyball, and many other kinds of sports.
5. Everyone _____ Amahl is in class today. She is absent.
6. What number is missing from this _____ ? 3, 6, 12, 15
7. The students are organizing a ping pong _____ . Sign up if you want to play.
8. Marie _____ from the Student Union to class because she was late.
9. In older elevators you have to push a button to make the elevator go. In new ones you just _____ the button.

10. Oscar told me some _____ news. He won a scholarship.
11. Walking and running are good _____ .
12. John _____ on a piece of paper that was on the floor.

C. Vocabulary Review
Match the words that are the opposite.

Column A

1. deliver _____
2. capture _____
3. straight _____
4. death _____
5. brave _____
6. loser _____
7. immediately _____
8. alive _____
9. kneel _____
10. national _____

Column B

a. later
b. stand up
c. international
d. winner
e. receive
f. goal
g. dead
h. let go
i. curved
j. smooth
k. afraid
l. life

D. Questions

1. Where is sumo wrestling popular?
2. What is a tournament?
3. Is sumo an old sport?
4. How are sumo wrestlers different from other athletes?
5. How do sumo wrestlers train?
6. Describe a sumo ring.
7. How does a sumo wrestler lose the match?
*8. Is sumo exciting?
*9. Is it good for a person to weigh 160 or 195 kilos?

E. Comprehension

1. Every year there are _____ sumo tournaments.
   a. 6
   b. 15
   c. 160
   d. 195

2. _____ says that there were sumo tournaments in the eighth century.
   a. A story   c. History
   b. An athlete   d. A wrestler

3. Most athletes are _____ .
   a. heavy   c. thin
   b. fat   d. smooth

4. Sumo wrestlers are _____ .
   a. straight   c. thin
   b. fat   d. smooth

5. Sumo is a _____ sport.
   a. fast   c. comfortable
   b. slow   d. silk

6. Sumo wrestlers _____ to make their bodies strong.
   a. eat   c. lose
   b. swing   d. exercise

7. Each wrestler tries to push the other _____ .
   a. down on the floor   c. into the air
   b. out of the ring   d. a and b

8. Japanese think that sumo is _____ .
   a. exciting   c. embarrassing
   b. boring   d. pleasant

F. Main Idea

1. Sumo wrestling between two fat men is a popular traditional sport in Japan.
2. The sumo wrestling ring is round and has a sand floor.
3. A sumo match is slow and the wrestlers are very fat.

TARAHUMARA FOOT RACES

5

The Tarahumara Indians live in the mountains in the state of Chihuahua in northern Mexico. This is an area of high mountains and deep tropical **valleys**. It sometimes snows in the mountains in winter. The
5 Indians live in caves, or in wooden or stone houses. They have small farms. There are not many roads.

Other Mexican Indians uses horses or **donkeys** for travel. The Tarahumaras walk **wherever** they need to go. They carry heavy baskets on their
10 **backs**. Perhaps this is why the Tarahumaras are **excellent** runners. They can run many kilometers without getting tired, and they like to organize **races**.

When the men race, they kick a wooden ball **ahead** of them while they run. Before they start
15 racing, they plan where and how long they will run. They might run just a few minutes or they might run for several hours. Sometimes they run in teams and sometimes each person runs as an **individual**.

The women's races are **similar** except that the
20 women do not kick a ball. They throw a wooden **hoop** in front of them with a stick. A hoop is a **ring** or circle.

The Tarahumaras have other games and sports. They even play a kind of lacrosse. However, the
25 Tarahumaras are famous because they can run so fast and so far.

low areas between mountains

wherever = anywhere

very good

running competitions

in front

one person

almost the same

UNUSUAL SPORTS

A. Vocabulary

excellent	ahead	runners	wherever
hoop	ring	valleys	donkeys
backs	similar	races	individual

1. Other Mexican Indians use horses or _____ for travel.
2. When the men race, they kick a wooden ball _____ of them while they run.
3. This is an area of high mountains and deep tropical _____ .
4. Perhaps this is why the Tarahumaras are _____ runners.
5. They carry heavy baskets on their _____ .
6. The women's races are _____ except that the women do not kick a ball.
7. They can run many kilometers without getting tired, and they like to organize _____ .
8. They throw a wooden _____ in front of them with a stick.
9. A hoop is a _____ or circle.
10. Sometimes they run in teams and sometimes each person runs as an _____ .
11. The Tarahumaras walk _____ they need to go.

B. Vocabulary (new context)

ring	valley	similar	donkeys
individually	backs	ahead	wherever
runners	excellent	caves	races

1. Some people like to go to car or horse _____ .
2. Mary likes jewelry. Yesterday she bought a gold _____ .
3. The kiwi and tern are both birds, but they are not _____ .
4. _____ can carry a lot on their _____ , but sometimes they are lazy.
5. As Betty and Pat drove along the highway, they could see beautiful mountains _____ of them.
6. A _____ is a low area between two mountains.
7. Sometimes students answer questions in a group, and sometimes they answer _____ .
8. Masako is an _____ student. She always gets good grades.
9. You will find English speakers _____ you go.

C. Vocabulary Review

weapon	drum	proud	elbow
handle	swept	yell	fields
net	speeding	touch	athletes
excited	series	exercise	except

1. Helen _____ the floor after she washed the dishes.
2. Some people fish with a hook and line. Others use a fish_____ .
3. Mr. and Mrs. Black have several_____ of corn on their farm.
4. You can open the desk drawer by pulling on the _____ .
5. There are_____ from several countries in the competition for the world cup.
6. The children were _____ when they went to Disneyland.
7. It is important to eat good food and get lots of _____ .
8. Tarahumaras play a _____ while they dance.
9. Do all of the exercises _____ the last one. Don't do that one.
10. The first unit in this book has a _____ of lessons on animals.
11. The police stopped me because I was _____ .

D. Questions

1. Where do the Tarahumaras live?
2. What is the land like there?
3. Does it ever snow?
4. Where do they get their food?
5. How do they travel?
6. How do most Mexican Indians travel?
7. Describe how the men race.
8. Do they always run in teams?
9. How is a women's race different from a men's race?
10. What is a hoop?
*11. Why are the Tarahumaras excellent runners?

E. Comprehension: True/False/No Information

_____ 1. Chihuahua is a state in Mexico.
_____ 2. It is hot in the valleys where the Tarahumaras live.
_____ 3. They buy all their food in stores.
_____ 4. Some of these Indians live in caves.
_____ 5. They cook their food outdoors.
_____ 6. The Tarahumara men are excellent runners but the women are not.
_____ 7. The winners of the races receive money.
_____ 8. They usually race down the mountains.
_____ 9. The women kick a ball as they race.
_____ 10. The Tarahumaras are famous because they play lacrosse.

F. Main Idea

1. The Tarahumaras live in caves and wooden and stone houses in the state of Chihuahua in Mexico.
2. The Tarahumaras are excellent runners and can race for several hours without getting tired.
3. The Tarahumara women's races are similar to the men's.

WORD STUDY

A. Map Study

1. These are the seven continents: Africa, Antarctica, Asia, Australia, Europe, North America, and South America. Tell what continent these places are on. Use the map on pages 260–261.

   a. Finland
   b. Egypt
   c. France
   d. Senegal
   e. Argentina
   f. Korea
   g. Burma
   h. Mount Everest
   i. Canada
   j. the South Pole

2. What countries are these places in? Use the map on pages 260–261.

   a. Chihuahua
   b. Sarawak
   c. Rome
   d. Hokkaido
   e. New Mexico
   f. Arizona
   g. Chicago
   h. Ontario
   i. Mindanao
   j. Naples

B. Compound Words

Make a compound word. Use a word from column A and a word from column B. Sometimes you can make two words.

Column A	Column B	
1. birth	a. mate	_____
2. table	b. how	_____
3. day	c. bell	_____
4. bed	d. cloth	_____
5. grass	e. light	_____
6. summer	f. land	_____
7. some	g. day	_____
8. door	h. time	_____
9. team	i. room	_____
10. sun	j. rise	_____

UNUSUAL SPORTS

C. Word Forms

	Verb	Noun	Adjective
1.		cube	cubic
2.	move	movement	
3.		ability	able
4.	free	freedom	free
5.	dry	dryer	dry
6.		nation	national
		nationality	
7.	excite	excitement	excited
8.	think	thought	
9.	run	running	
		runner	
10.	please	pleasure	pleasant
			pleased

Put the correct word form in the blanks. Use a word from line 1 in sentence 1, and so on. Use the right verb forms and singular and plural nouns.

1. What is a _____ ? What does a _____ gram of water weigh?
2. A zipper _____ up and down. Each _____ opens or closes the hooks.
3. A water spider has the _____ to live underwater. It is _____ to do this because it takes air bubbles with it.
4. The Burmese captured Naresuen. He won his _____ by boxing. Then he was _____ . He returned to Thailand.
5. You can _____ your clothes in a clothes _____ . When they are _____ , take them out.
6. Where are you from? What is your _____ ? What does your _____ flag look like?
7. My cousin's family went to Disney World in Florida. The children were very _____ . They got tired from all the _____ .
8. What are you _____ about? Is your family in your _____ often?
9. Tom _____ five kilometers every morning. He is a fast _____ . _____ is good for him.
10. This is a _____ city. I am _____ to be here.

D. Past Tense Review
Write the past of these verbs.

1. step	6. speak	11. think
2. mix	7. try	12. grow
3. keep	8. meet	13. lose
4. lead	9. pay	14. drip
5. build	10. sell	15. send

E. Irregular Verbs
Memorize these verbs. Then use the past tense of each verb in a sentence.

Simple	Past	Simple	Past
a. drive	drove	f. slide	slid
b. sweep	swept	g. catch	caught
c. drink	drank	h. feel	felt
d. fly	flew	i. forget	forgot
e. hear	heard	j. run	ran

F. Context Clues
Some words have more than one meaning. Decide what the word means in each sentence.

1. We saw a good **show** at the Student Union last night. The name of it was "Star Wars."
   a. look at
   b. let someone look at
   c. movie
   d. television program

2. We **store** our winter clothes in the garage during the summer.
   a. keep
   b. throw away
   c. a place to buy something
   d. a place for a car

3. During the month of Ramadan, Muslims **fast** during the day, and they eat at night. They get very hungry during the day.
   a. quickly
   b. don't eat
   c. soon
   d. don't be slow

4. What is the **date** today?
   a. a kind of fruit
   b. a kind of palm tree
   c. the day of the month
   d. the name of the day

5. David couldn't see the soccer game yesterday. He had problems with his car. When he arrived at the field, the game was **all over**.
   a. started
   b. finished
   c. everywhere
   d. nowhere

6. Stan **leaves for** work at 7:15 every morning.
   a. goes to
   b. jumps
   c. things that grow on trees
   d. the opposite of *dies*

7. You must **sign** your name on every check that you write.
   a. the language for deaf people
   b. something to tell drivers what to do
   c. write
   d. read

8. A pencil is very **light**.
   a. the opposite of dark
   b. the opposite of heavy
   c. white
   d. new

VOCABULARY

A

able 177
about 6
above 14
accept 201
across 143
add 89
adult 115
adventure 186
afraid 10
age 148
ago 57
agree 157
ahead 244
alive 14
all over 6
alone 124
already 41
also 6
ambassador 173
among 157
apart 197
appear 124
aquarium 18
area 124
army 85
around 69
arrest 186
arrive 157
art 57
artificial 97
aside 240
at all 120
athlete 240
attend 143
avalanche 177
axe 148

B

back 244
bake 100
ballpoint 205
bamboo 148
basket 57
battle 227
be able 177
beak 3
bear 10
beard 143
become 61

believe 18
bell 129
belong to 182
below 115
bend 197
beside 14
better 61
blow 93
boring 93
both 45
bottle 97
brave 186
breathe 14
broom 65
bubble 93
burn 57
button 29
by himself 186

C

caffeine 97
camel 6
can 97
canoe 169
captain 232
capture 227
carbon dioxide 97
card 100
carry 29
catch 10
cattle 152
cave 148
century 89
cheap 37
chew 93
chicle 93
choose 177
claw 120
climate 210
climb 29
cloth 148
cloud 33
club 177
coal 205
coast 115
collect 37
colony 157
comfortable 140
common 100
company 89

competition 158
complete 143
computer 152
continue 144
cool 6
could 29
cover 111
crop 61
cross 201
cubic 214
curling 232
current 169
curve 232

D

dance 45
dangerous 97
dark 115
date 57
dead 152
deaf 45
death 183
decide 214
deep 139
defeat 182
deliver 201
describe 6
desert 6
difficult 45
dig 111
dip 205
dirt 111
disease 61
distance 214
dolphin 18
donkey 244
double 169
dozen 197
drip 97
drum 227
during 3

E

each other 45
ear 85
earn 73
earth 33
eastern 65
either 97
elbow 227

GRAMMAR

IRREGULAR VERBS

Simple	Past	Simple	Past
be	was, were	hear	heard
become	became	hit	hit
begin	began	hurt	hurt
blow	blew	keep	kept
bring	brought	know	knew
build	built	lead	led
buy	bought	leave	left
catch	caught	lose	lost
choose	chose	make	made
come	came	meet	met
cut	cut	pay	paid
do (does)	did	put	put
drink	drank	ring	rang
drive	drove	run	ran
eat	ate	see	saw
fall	fell	sell	sold
feel	felt	send	sent
fight	fought	sleep	slept
find	found	slide	slid
fly	flew	speak	spoke
forget	forgot	spend	spent
freeze	froze	sweep	swept
get	got	take	took
give	gave	teach	taught
go (goes)	went	tell	told
grow	grew	think	thought
have (has)	had	understand	understood
		wear	wore
		win	won
		write	wrote